IN THEIR OWN WORDS

IN THEIR OWN WORDS

*The Testimonies of Martin Luther,
John Calvin, John Knox,
and John Bunyan*

David B. Calhoun

THE BANNER OF TRUTH TRUST

THE BANNER OF TRUTH TRUST

Head Office
3 Murrayfield Road
Edinburgh
EH12 6EL
UK

North America Sales
PO Box 621
Carlisle
PA 17013
USA

banneroftruth.org

First published 2018
© David B. Calhoun 2018

*

ISBN
Print: 978 1 84871 837 1
EPUB: 978 1 84871 838 8
Kindle: 978 1 84871 839 5

*

Typeset in 11/15 Adobe Garamond Pro
at The Banner of Truth Trust, Edinburgh

Printed in the USA by
Versa Press Inc.,
East Peoria, IL.

Contents

Testimonies

Testimonies are found throughout the Bible. They appear in the historical books of the Old Testament, especially in Ezra and Nehemiah. The testimony of David can be gathered from his Psalms. Testimonies of the prophets are found in the books of Habakkuk and Jonah, as well as in briefer passages in Isaiah, Jeremiah, Ezekiel, and elsewhere. The apostle Paul gives his testimony twice in Acts 20–26.

The best-known testimony in the early church is Augustine's *Confessions*. Garry Wills argues that the proper English rendering of '*Confessions*' is not the familiar and obvious one, but rather '*The Testimony*', the title of his biography of Augustine. In his testimony, Augustine confesses his sin, but even more he confesses God's grace, mercy, and goodness to him. Like Augustine's *Confessions*, the testimonies of Martin Luther, John Calvin, John Knox, and John Bunyan illustrate the truth stated by Paul that 'where sin increased, grace abounded all the more, so that as sin reigned in death, grace also might reign through righteousness leading to eternal life through Jesus Christ our Lord' (Rom. 5:20-21).

There are hundreds of biographies of Luther, Calvin, Knox, and Bunyan, and hundreds of thousands of pages describing their times and explaining their teaching. There is something to be gained, however, in listening to these men tell their stories in their own words. I have gathered testimonial statements from Luther, Calvin, Knox, and Bunyan. I seldom add criticism. I don't need to. Luther, Calvin, Knox, and Bunyan are candid in confessing their own sins and failures.

I have edited the quotations, modernizing the language where it was felt necessary, but I have been careful not to alter the meaning or emphasis of the original. I have added brief comments to provide background and context. I have not included the five or six hundred endnotes identifying the sources of the quotations. Some of these sources are indicated in the text. Many of the others can be found in the information provided in one of the early endnotes for each chapter.

David B. Calhoun
July 2018

I

Martin Luther's Testimony

'Be it at home or on the pulpit, at the lectern or the desk, as an authority on politics or pamphleteer, [Luther's] personal experience is always present,' writes Heiko Oberman.[1] Luther's testimony is found in his sermons and treatises, commentaries, letters, and especially in the preface to his Latin works and in the *Table Talk*, a collection of Luther's conversation, during the years 1531 to 1544, with dinner guests in his house, the former Augustinian monastery in Wittenberg.[2] Here Luther was at his best in honest, down-to-earth, moving, sharp, generous, occasionally vulgar, and often humorous comments. Thomas Carlyle believed that in Luther's *Table Talk* we have 'many beautiful unconscious displays of the man, and what sort of nature he had'.[3]

'My father was a poor miner.'

Martin Luther was born on November 10, 1483, in Eisleben, Germany. His parents, Hans and Margarethe Luder (Martin changed the name to Luther), were impoverished hard-working people. 'My father was a poor miner,' Luther said; 'my mother carried all her wood home on her back.' Luther's parents sought, with some success, to better their situation in life, but it was never easy.

Luther's father and mother did not hesitate to punish him physically, sometimes harshly. 'My father once whipped me so severely,' Luther said, 'that I ran away from him, and he was worried that he might not win me back again.' For stealing a nut, Luther's mother thrashed him so that she drew blood. When Luther himself became a father, he said, 'One should not hit children too hard, but deal with them more gently as God does.' But the beatings he received at home, Luther believed, were well intentioned. 'My father certainly meant heartily by me,' he said. He recalled affectionately a little ditty his mother sang,

> If folk don't like you and me,
> the fault with us is like to be!

Luther's early schooling was not outstanding, but he went on to earn the Baccalaureate and Master's degrees at the University of Erfurt, 'one of the most dynamic faculties in Europe'.[4] Luther was ecstatic. He said, 'I contend that there is no temporal or worldly joy to compare with it!' He then began to study law at Erfurt with his father's blessing.

'Help me, St Anne! I will become a monk.'

In the summer of 1505 Luther was walking back to Erfurt after visiting his parents when he was suddenly caught in a terrible thunderstorm. Knocked to the ground by lightning, he cried out to St Anne, supposed to be the Virgin Mary's mother, and the patron saint of miners, as well as the helper of people in distress in thunderstorms, 'Help me, St Anne! I will become a monk.'

Two weeks later, just before he turned twenty-two, Luther entered the Augustinian monastery in Erfurt. He wrote to his father that the thunderstorm and his vow to become a monk were the will of God. Hans Luther, who was expecting Martin to support him and his wife in their old age, angrily answered that it might well have been the work of the devil! Later Hans changed his mind, at least temporarily, and praised Martin for his decision and wished him well. But it wasn't long before Hans was again criticizing his son. When Luther celebrated his first Mass, he asked his father why he was so angry about the step he had taken. Hans replied reproachfully, 'Don't you know that it's written, Honour your father and your mother?'

Luther came to believe that Hans had been right when he said that perhaps his son did not hear the voice of God in the thunderstorm but that of the devil. Luther wrote to his father, 'You quickly came back with a reply so fitting and so much to the point that I have scarcely in my entire life heard any man say anything that struck me so forcibly and stayed with me so long.' Luther believed that his decision to become a monk was wrong because it was made against his father's will and out of fear, but he admitted, 'How much good the merciful Lord has allowed to come of it.' His experience as a monk convinced him that this was not a sure path to heaven, as many people believed.

'I was a good monk.'

Luther was determined to fulfil completely the demands of the monastic life—and even to go beyond what was required. He said, 'I was a good monk, and I kept the rule of my order so strictly that I may say that if ever a monk got to heaven by his monkery it was I.' He confessed his sins frequently, often daily, and for as long as six hours on a single occasion. Because he took up so much of their time, no confessor wanted to have anything to do with him. Luther said: 'When I was a monk, I was unwilling to omit any of the prayers [prescribed for certain hours of the day], but when I was busy with lecturing and writing I often accumulated my appointed prayers for a whole week, or even two or three weeks. Then I would take a Saturday off, or shut myself in for as long as three days without food and drink, until I had said the prescribed prayers. This made my head split, and as a consequence I couldn't close my eyes for five nights, lay sick unto death, and went out of my senses. I almost fasted myself to death, for again and again I went for three days without taking a drop of water or a morsel of food. I was very serious about it.'

Despite all his efforts to earn God's favour, Luther could not believe that God was willing to forgive him. 'In the monastery,' he said, 'I did not think about women, money, or possessions; instead my heart trembled and fidgeted about whether God would bestow his grace on me.'

'If it had not been for Dr Staupitz I would have sunk into hell.'

'If it had not been for Dr Staupitz,' Luther said, 'I would have sunk into hell.'

Johannes von Staupitz, who became vicar general of the German Augustinian Observants, was one of the key figures of early Reformation history. 'Staupitz laid all the foundations,' Luther said. He helped the zealous monk through his darkest times. 'Through Staupitz, the Lord Jesus repeatedly uplifted and strengthened me in the most wonderful way,' Luther wrote. 'I recall that at the beginning of my cause Dr Staupitz said to me: "It pleases me that the doctrine which you preach ascribes the glory and everything to God alone and nothing to man; for to God (who is clearer than the sun) one cannot ascribe too much glory and goodness." This word comforted and strengthened me greatly at the time.'

Again and again Staupitz told Luther that in his fears and doubts he must keep his eyes fixed 'on that man who is called Christ'. Luther learned that lesson well. He later advised a woman who was worried that she was not one of God's elect, 'The highest of all God's commands is this, that we hold up before our eyes the image of his dear son, our Lord Jesus Christ. Every day he should be the excellent mirror wherein we behold how much God loves us and how well, in his infinite goodness, he has cared for us.'

When Staupitz chose to remain in the Roman Catholic Church, Luther felt deserted and even betrayed. He wrote to his friend, 'You seem to me a very different Staupitz from the one who used to preach grace and the cross.' But a year before his own death, Luther praised Staupitz for 'first of all being my father in this doctrine, and having given birth to me in Christ'.

'Who can bear the majesty of God?'

Luther was ordained in the spring of 1507 and celebrated his first Mass a month later. He recalled: 'When at length I stood before the altar I was so terrified by the words "to thee, the eternal, living, and true God" that I thought of running away from the altar.' He 'felt like fleeing from the world like Judas'. 'Who can bear the majesty of God without Christ as Mediator?' he asked.

Years later, lecturing on Genesis, Luther said: 'A prayer which breaks through the clouds and reaches up to the majesty of God is not easy. I, ashes, dust, and full of sin, speak with the living, eternally true God. This cannot but cause one to tremble, as I did when I celebrated my first Mass.

Joyous faith, however, which rests on the mercy and the word of God overcomes the fear of his majesty and rises boldly above it.'

'Who knows if it is really true?'

In 1510 Luther was sent to Rome on monastery business, delighted that such an important pilgrimage would add to his list of good works. In Rome he visited holy sites and celebrated Mass daily. 'There is a saying in Rome, "Blessed is the mother whose son celebrates a Mass in St Giovanni in Laterano on a Saturday",' Luther wrote. 'How I would have loved to make my mother blessed there! But the waiting line was too long, and I did not get a turn.' To free his grandfather from purgatory, Luther climbed the Scala Sancta on his knees, saying the Lord's Prayer on each step. When he reached the top he asked, 'Who knows if it is really true?' Luther was deeply troubled when he realized, as Oberman puts it, that 'God's grace was for sale in Rome.'⁵ 'I wouldn't have believed it if I hadn't seen it for myself,' Luther said. 'For so great and shameless is the godlessness and wickedness there that neither God nor man, neither sin nor disgrace are taken seriously.' Luther summed up his experience in Rome with a proverb for a bad deal: 'I was so foolish as to carry onions to Rome and bring back garlic.' But his experience in Rome, like his life as a monk, further convinced him that something was seriously wrong with the Roman Catholic Church. Luther said, 'I wouldn't take a hundred thousand gulden in exchange for what I saw and heard in Rome, for otherwise I'd always be afraid that I was doing the pope an injustice. I speak of what I've seen.'

The Bible is 'a mighty tree and every word a little branch'.

In 1512 Luther received his doctoral degree in theology. He said, 'In Erfurt only fifty-year-olds were made doctors of theology. Many took umbrage at my getting the doctorate at the age of twenty-eight,' but 'Staupitz drove me to it.' Staupitz held the chair of biblical theology at the University of Wittenberg until he turned it over to Luther, who filled it for the rest of his life.

For several years Luther had taught philosophy to the younger monks, but he came to feel that philosophy was like waiting for the real thing. Theology, he said, 'penetrates to the kernel of the nut, the germ of the wheat, and the marrow of the bones'. Luther found it 'more than astonishing that our scholars can so brazenly claim that Aristotle does not contradict Catholic truth'. 'The whole of Aristotle is to theology as shadow is to light,' he said. 'That's the way human nature is, asking Why? Why? Why? This is what happens when philosophy is introduced into theology. When the devil went to Eve with the question Why? the game was up. One should be on one's guard against this. It's better to fall on one's knees and pray an "Our Father".'

Luther began to lecture at the University of Wittenberg on the Bible—the Psalms, followed by Romans, Galatians, Hebrews, and the Psalms again. He read through the Bible twice every year. It is 'alive', Luther said, 'it speaks to me. It has feet, it runs after me. It has hands, it lays hold of me.' 'If you picture the Bible to be a mighty tree and every word a little branch,' he said, 'I have shaken every one of these branches because I wanted to know what it was and what it meant.'

'I felt myself to be reborn, and to have gone through open doors into paradise.'

One of the branches of Scripture that Luther shook long and hard was Romans 1:17—'For therein [in the gospel] is the righteousness of God revealed.'[6] Those words struck Luther's conscience like lightning.

'When I heard them I was exceedingly terrified. If God is righteous, he must punish sin.'

'I did not love, yes, I hated the righteous God who punishes sinners. Nevertheless, I beat importunately upon Paul at that place [Rom. 1:17], most ardently desiring to know what St Paul wanted.'

'At last, by the mercy of God, meditating day and night, I gave heed to the context of the words, namely, "In it the righteousness of God is revealed, as it is written, he who through faith is righteous shall live." I began to understand that the righteousness of God is that by which the righteous lives by a gift of God, namely by faith.'

'The justice of God is that righteousness by which through grace and sheer mercy God justifies us through faith. Our salvation is not based on our righteousness, our merit, but on God's mercy. My spirit was thereby cheered. For it's by the righteousness of God that we're justified and saved through Christ.'

'Thereupon I felt myself to be reborn, and to have gone through open doors into paradise. The whole of Scripture took on a new meaning, and whereas before the "justice of God" had filled me with hate, now it became to me inexpressibly sweet in greater love. This passage of Paul became to me a gate to heaven. Later I read Augustine's *The Spirit and the Letter*, where contrary to hope I found that he, too, interpreted God's righteousness in a similar way, as the righteousness with which God clothes us when he justifies us.'

'My son, be of good cheer; your sins are forgiven you.'

Luther spent the rest of his life struggling to grasp more fully the wonder and full meaning of justification by faith. In 1538 he said, 'I have preached for twenty-five years and still don't understand the verse "He who through faith is righteous shall live."' Luther said, 'If I could believe that God was not angry with me, I would stand on my head with joy.' Luther could not fully grasp this great truth, but he believed it with all his heart. 'I did not learn my theology all at once,' Luther wrote, 'but I had to search deeper for it where my trials and temptations took me. Living, nay rather dying and being damned made me a theologian, not understanding, reading or speculation.'

In a letter to a troubled friend, he joyfully wrote about the good news that he had found in the gospel, 'Therefore, my sweet brother, learn Christ and him crucified; despairing of yourself, learn to pray to him, saying, "You, Lord Jesus, are my righteousness, but I am your sin; you have taken on yourself what you were not and have given to me what I was not."'

The gospel of God's grace clearly and beautifully fills Luther's prayers. 'Dear Lord Jesus, I feel my sins. They bite and gnaw and frighten me. Where shall I go? I look to you, Lord Jesus, and believe in you. Although my faith is weak, I cling to you and am made sure, for you have promised: who believes in me shall have eternal life. Even if my conscience is troubled and my sins frighten me and make me tremble, you have still said: "My son, be of good cheer; your sins are forgiven you. I will raise you up on the last day, and you will have eternal life." I cannot help myself by my own strength. I come to you for help. Amen.'

In his hymns Luther sang his testimony, as in this paraphrase of Psalm 130, written, with the music, in 1523, several years after his discovery of God's justifying grace.

From depths of woe I raise to thee
   The voice of lamentation;
Lord, turn a gracious ear to me
   And hear my supplication:
If thou iniquities dost mark,
   Our secret sins and misdeeds dark,
O who shall stand before thee?

To wash away the crimson stain,
   Grace, grace alone availeth;
Our works, alas! are all in vain;
   In much the best life faileth:
No man can glory in thy sight,
   All must alike confess thy might,
And live alone by mercy.

Therefore my trust is in the Lord,
   And not in mine own merit;
On him my soul shall rest, his word
   Upholds my fainting spirit:
His promised mercy is my fort,
   My comfort, and my sweet support;
I wait for it with patience.

Though great our sins and sore our woes,
   His grace much more aboundeth;
His helping love no limit knows,
   Our utmost need it soundeth.
Our Shepherd good and true is he,
   Who will at last his Israel free
From all their sin and sorrow.

'The true treasure of the church is the most holy gospel of the glory and grace of God.'

'When in the year 1517 indulgences were sold in these regions for most shameful gain,' Luther wrote, 'I was then a young preacher, a young doctor of theology, and I began to dissuade the people and to urge them not to listen to the clamours of the indulgence hawkers. I took steps only gradually against the impudent Tetzel, but everybody ventured to defend him.' Luther was sure that 'the pope would damn Tetzel and bless me', but instead of blessings from Rome he received 'thunder and lightning'.

On the eve of All Saints' Day, October 31, 1517, Luther, 'out of love and zeal for truth and the desire to bring it to light', posted ninety-five theses, probably on the door of the Castle Church in Wittenberg. This document proposed a 'disputation on the power and efficacy of indulgences'. Some of Luther's theses went beyond that issue, stating his developing views on the whole of medieval doctrine, especially the following. These, too, are words of testimony.

'When our Lord and Master Jesus Christ said "Repent!" (Matt. 4:17), he willed the entire life of believers to be one of repentance.'

'The true treasure of the church is the most holy gospel of the glory and grace of God.'

'Christians should be exhorted to be diligent in following Christ, their head, through penalties, death, and hell; and thus be confident of entering into heaven through many tribulations rather than through the false security of peace (Acts 14:22).'

'I am expecting the curses of Rome any day.'

For the next few years Luther was summoned to meetings, hearings, and trials, where he repeated, explained, and defended his views. Despite periods of worry and fear, he did so with faith and courage. 'I am expecting the curses of Rome any day,' he wrote to a friend. 'I have everything in readiness. When they come, I am girded like Abraham to go I know not where, but sure of this, that God is everywhere.'

At a gathering of Augustinians in Heidelberg in April 1518, Luther presented twenty-eight theses. Luther's preface and the theses themselves contain notes of his own spiritual experience. Luther told his Augustinian brothers that we must distrust 'completely our own wisdom' and rely on 'St Paul, the especially chosen vessel and instrument of Christ' and also 'St Augustine, his most trustworthy interpreter'.

Thesis 1 states: 'The law of God, although the soundest doctrine of life, is not able to bring man to righteousness but rather stands in the way.'

Thesis 18 reads: 'It is certain that man must utterly despair of his own ability before he is prepared to receive the grace of Christ.'

Thesis 25 states: 'He is not righteous who does much, but he who, without work, believes much in Christ.'

Thesis 26 asserts that 'the law says, "Do this", and it is never done. Grace says, "Believe in this", and everything is already done.'

Thesis 28 sums it all up: 'The love of God does not find, but creates, that which is pleasing to it.'

These statements reveal Luther's deepening understanding of the gospel of God's grace, and reflect his testimony of experiencing that grace in his own life.

'So I came to Augsburg, afoot and poor.'

In October 1518 Luther went to Augsburg to be examined by Cardinal Cajetan. 'So I came to Augsburg,' he wrote, 'afoot and poor.' Luther expected the worst. 'Oh, the disgrace I shall bring down upon my parents,' he thought. But then he added, 'May Christ live, may Martin die—like every sinner.' When Luther was asked whether he believed Prince Frederick the Wise would take up arms to defend him, he replied, 'This I do not at all desire.' 'And where will you stay?' he was asked. Luther answered, 'Under heaven.'

In July 1519 Luther went to Leipzig to debate with Roman Catholic scholar John Eck. Luther said that by then he had 'read and taught the sacred Scriptures most diligently, privately and publicly for seven years, so that I knew them nearly all by memory. I had also acquired the beginning of the knowledge of Christ and faith in him, that is, not by works but by faith in Christ are we made righteous and saved. I had already defended the proposition publicly that the pope is not the head of the church by divine right. Nevertheless, I did not draw the conclusion that the pope must be of the devil. For what is not of God must of necessity be of the devil.'

When pressed to state his views clearly, Luther answered, 'God once spoke through the mouth of an ass. I will tell you straight what I think, I am a Christian theologian; and I am bound, not only to assert, but to defend the truth with my blood and death. I want to believe freely and be a slave to the authority of no one, whether council, university, or pope.'

In a letter to a friend who was fearful that Luther might give way in the face of constant threats and dangers, Luther assured him that whatever his inner fears and doubts, he would never forsake the cause. 'You ask how I am getting on. I do not know. Satan was never so furious against me. I can say this, that I have never sought goods, honour, and glory, and I am not cast down by the hostility of the masses. In fact, the more they rage the more I am filled with the Spirit. But, and this may surprise you, I am scarcely able to resist the smallest wave of inner despair, and that is why the least tremor of this kind expels the greatest of the other sort. You need not fear that I shall desert the standards.'

'This is wonderful news to believe that salvation lies outside ourselves.'

In the summer and fall of 1520 Luther wrote three important treatises—*Address to the Christian Nobility of the German Nation*; *The Babylonian Captivity of the Church*; and *On the Freedom of a Christian*. In the last he wrote words that eloquently expressed his own testimony: 'This is wonderful news to believe that salvation lies outside ourselves. I am justified and acceptable to God, although there are in me sin, unrighteousness, and horror of death. Yet I must look elsewhere and see no sin. This is wonderful, not to see what I see, not to feel what I feel. Before my eyes I see a gulden, or a sword, or a fire, and I must say, "There is no gulden, no sword, no fire." The forgiveness of sins is like this.'

'When God in his sheer mercy and without any merit of mine has given me such unspeakable riches, shall I not then freely, joyously, wholeheartedly, unprompted, do everything that I know will please him? I will give myself as a sort of Christ to my neighbour as Christ gave himself for me.'

'I did nothing. The word did everything.'

When he began his work of reforming the church Luther said that at first he was 'like a drowning man, tossed about in the waves. Now I've fought my way through. I see that I tried to bring impossible contradictions into harmony. It was a wretched patchwork.' On another occasion he remarked that he had been led 'like a horse with blinders on'. But gradually he learned that the Reformation was God's work. He said, 'I simply taught, preached, and wrote God's word. And while I slept or drank Wittenberg beer with my friends Philip and Amsdorf, the word so greatly weakened the papacy that no prince or emperor ever inflicted such losses on it. I did nothing. The word did everything.'

'If God is for us, who can be against us?'

On June 12, 1520, Luther's writings were condemned by the papal bull of Pope Leo X that was introduced with the words, 'Arise, O Lord, and judge your cause. A wild boar has invaded your vineyard.' Luther experienced moments of despair as well as outbursts of rage, but his prevailing mood was expressed in a letter to a troubled minister.

'Our warfare is not with flesh and blood, but against spiritual wickedness in the heavenly places, against the world rulers of this darkness. Let us then stand firm and heed the trumpet of the Lord. Satan is fighting, not against us, but against Christ in us. We fight the battles of the Lord. Be strong therefore. If God is for us, who can be against us? You are dismayed because Eck is publishing a most severe bull against Luther, his books, and his followers. Whatever may happen, I am not moved, because nothing can happen save in accord with the will of him who sits upon the [throne of] heaven directing all. Let not your hearts be troubled. Your Father knows your need before you ask him.

MARTIN LUTHER'S TESTIMONY

Not a leaf from a tree falls to the ground without his knowledge. How much less can any of us fall unless it be his will.'

On December 10, sixty days after he had received it, accompanied by a large crowd of his fellow professors and students, Luther burned the papal bull, as well as books of church law, and Eck's writings. Sixty days after he received the papal bull, Luther burned it, as well as books of church law and Eck's writings. On January 3, 1521, he was excommunicated.

'Here I stand, God help me.'

Luther was determined to go to the Diet of Worms in 1521 despite the danger. He wrote to a friend, 'We shall enter Worms, even if all the gates of hell and all the powers of heaven try to prevent it.' But he was not without feelings of despondency and fear. The morning before he appeared before the Diet, he prayed:

'Oh God, Oh God, Oh my God, stand by me, against all the wisdom and reason of the world. Do it. You alone must do it. It is not really my concern; it is yours. Alone I have nothing to do with these great lords of the world. I want good and quiet days, undisturbed. But it is your cause; it is righteous and eternal. Stand by me. Oh true and eternal God. I do not rely on human counsel, for it would be in vain. Stand by me, O God, in the name of your dear Son, Jesus Christ, who shall be my defence and shelter, yes, my mighty fortress, through the might and strength of your Holy Spirit. Amen.'

As the trial continued, Luther grew stronger. He boldly insisted on absolute obedience to the Bible against all authorities, popes or councils, and concluded with these memorable words: 'Unless I am convinced by the testimony of the Scriptures or by clear reason (for I do not trust either in the pope or in councils alone, since it is well known that they have often erred and contradicted themselves), I am bound to Scriptures I have quoted and my conscience is captive to the word of God. I cannot and I will not retract anything, since it is neither safe nor right to go against conscience. I cannot do otherwise. Here I stand, God help me.'

Luther's teaching was formally condemned by the Edict of Worms and he was put under the ban of the Holy Roman Empire. 'Three times have I been excommunicated,' Luther said. 'The first time was by Dr Staupitz who absolved me from the observance and rule of the Augustinian Order so that if the pope pressed him to imprison me or command me to be silent, he could excuse himself on the ground that I was not under his observance. The second time was by the pope and the third time was by the emperor [at the Diet of Worms].' But, said Luther, 'the Lord took me up'.

'I was imprisoned in my Patmos, high up in the fortress in the kingdom of the birds.'

As Luther made his way home to Wittenberg he was suddenly taken by friends and whisked away to the safety of the Wartburg Castle. Roland Bainton describes what Luther experienced when he came to the castle: 'As he laid him down in the chamber of the almost untenanted bastion, and the owls and bats wheeled about in the darkness, it seemed to him that the devil was pelting nuts at the ceiling and rolling casks down the stairs. More insidious than such pranks of the prince of darkness was the unallayed question, "Are you alone wise? Have so many centuries gone wrong? What if you are in error and are taking so many others with you to eternal damnation?" In the morning he threw open the casement window and looked out on the fair Thuringian hills. In the distance he could see a cloud of smoke rising from the pits of the charcoal burners. A gust of wind lifted and dissipated the cloud. Even so were his doubts dispelled and his faith restored.'[7]

But Luther's fears and doubts did not leave him for long. He struggled with temptations and sin. He wrote to his colleague and friend Philip Melanchthon: 'I sit here at ease, hardened and unfeeling—alas! praying little, grieving little for the church of God, burning rather in the fierce fires of my untamed flesh. It comes to this: I should be afire in the spirit; in reality I am afire in the flesh, with lust, laziness, idleness, sleepiness. Pray for me, I beg you, for in my seclusion here I am submerged in sins.'

Luther wrote, 'I was often pestered by the devil when I was imprisoned in my Patmos, high up in the fortress in the kingdom of the birds. I resisted him in faith and confronted him with this verse: God who created man, is mine, and all things are under his feet. If you have any power over him, try it!'

'I have begun the Bible translation although the task far exceeds my powers.'

Luther felt useless, but soon found something to do. He wrote several treatises, including a *Commentary on the Magnificat*, and began work on a translation of the New Testament into German. 'I have begun the Bible translation although the task far exceeds my powers,' he wrote. But Luther worked quickly, translating the entire New Testament in eleven weeks. It was published in September 1522 and is known as the *September Testament*. A dozen Septembers later, the complete German Bible appeared, translated by Luther from the best available Greek and Hebrew texts, into the lively everyday language of the people. Luther said, 'One must ask the mother at home, the children in the street, the man in the market, and listen to how they speak, and translate accordingly. That way they will understand and notice that one is speaking German to them.'

The German Bible, according to Roland Bainton, was Luther's 'noblest achievement'.[8] He worked on it for the rest of his life. Before dinner every Wednesday and Thursday, from the summer of 1539 to the beginning of 1541, Luther assembled a group of scholars, his 'Sanhedrin' he called it, to assist him in revising his translation of the Old Testament.

The last printed page on which he ever looked was the proof of the latest revision of his New Testament.

Luther said: 'It was my intention and hope, when I began to translate the Bible into German, that there should be less writing of other books and instead more studying and reading of the Scriptures. As happened to the book of Deuteronomy in the times of the kings of Judah, the pure knowledge of the divine word has been lost, so that the Bible lies forgotten in the dust under the bench. It behooves us to let the prophets and apostles stand at the professor's lectern, while we, down below at their feet, listen to what they say. It is not they who must hear what we say.'

'I was disturbed that the gospel was brought into disrepute at Wittenberg.'

During his stay at the Wartburg Luther was greatly disturbed by reports of what was happening in Wittenberg at the hands of his more radical reforming friends. Despite the imperial ban, and against the clear instructions of his prince, Luther left the Wartburg Castle and returned to Wittenberg on March 6, 1522. He explained in a letter to Frederick the Wise: 'I was disturbed that the gospel was brought into disrepute at Wittenberg. If I were not sure that the gospel is on our side, I would have given up. All the sorrow I have had is nothing compared to this. I have done enough for Your Grace by staying in hiding for a year. I would have you know that I come to Wittenberg with a higher protection than that of Your Grace. You are excused if I am captured or killed. If Your Grace had eyes, you would see the glory of God.'

Luther set about restoring peace and order in Wittenberg. He successfully pleaded for patience. 'Give men time. I took three years of constant study, reflection, and discussion to arrive where I now am, and can the common man, untutored in such matters, be expected to move the same distance in three months? Such haste and violence betray a lack of confidence in God. See how much he has been able to accomplish through me, though I did no more than pray and preach. The word did it all.'

'I wouldn't give up my Katie for France or for Venice.'

Luther wrote to a friend, 'Suddenly, unexpectedly, and while my mind was on other matters, the Lord has snared me with the yoke of marriage.' On June 13, 1525, Luther married Katharina von Bora, a former nun, a handsome woman of noble descent, fifteen years younger than he was. Luther said that he married in order to 'please his father, tease the pope, and vex the devil'.

'No sweeter thing than love of woman—may a man be so fortunate,' Luther wrote in the margin beside Proverbs 31 in his German translation. 'God blessed me with the happiest marriage,' said Luther. 'I wouldn't give up my Katie for France or for Venice.' He called his beloved Epistle to the Galatians 'my Katie von Bora'.

Luther loved Katie and he valued her help. She ran their household, relieving Martin of many time-consuming duties. 'It is a good thing that God came to my aid and gave me a wife,' Luther said. Katie planted a large garden, operated her own brewery, and treated her husband's many illnesses with skill. Her husband dubbed her 'the morning star of Wittenberg', as her day began at 4:00 a.m. She cared for the steady stream of relatives, students, and visitors to their Wittenberg home, creating 'a model for the Lutheran household in centuries to come'.[9]

Luther recognized in Katie 'his principal support in this world ... His marriage with her was the single greatest new influence on his life and thinking after the monastery.'[10] A short time before he died, he asked his gathered friends to comfort Katie, who 'served me not only as a wife but as my assistant'. When Luther made his will in 1542 he praised Katie as 'a pious and faithful spouse' who 'has at all times held me dear'. He was especially careful to assure Katie's future, because under Saxon inheritance laws she would have received little.

In his Genesis commentary Luther wrote, 'With the woman who has been joined to me by God I may jest, have fun, and converse more pleasantly.' But for Luther a good marriage was more than fun. It involved intellectual companionship and required mutual forgiving and forgetting. Luther and his wife were both realistic about marriage and about each other. He admitted that Katie had 'some shortcomings' but that they were 'outweighed by a great many virtues'. Luther teased her, and occasionally spoke sharply to her or about her, but she seemed to take it all in good spirits. He was no doubt laughing when he said, 'If I ever have to find myself a wife again, I will hew myself an obedient wife out of stone.'

'I'm rich, my God has given me a nun and has added three children.'

Luther believed that marriage was 'a divinely noble business'.[11] So were children. 'I'm rich,' Luther said in 1532, 'my God has given me a nun and has added three children.' Katie and Martin had three more children after that. Luther was nearly forty-three at the birth of their first child, Hans, and fifty-two when Margaret, their youngest, was born. Luther took delight in his children; they were a 'most beautiful joy'. Playing with one of his babies, Luther said, 'Oh, this is the best of God's blessings.' When neighbours sniggered at Luther washing children's diapers, he declared, 'Let them laugh. God and the angels are smiling in heaven.'

Luther wrote that every father should 'regard his child as nothing else but an eternal treasure God has commanded him to protect, and so prevent the world, the flesh, and the devil from stealing the child away and bringing him to destruction'. Luther regularly conducted family devotions with his wife and children. In his *Preface to the German Mass*, Luther wrote, 'Christ to train men, had to become man himself. If we wish to train children, we must become children with them.' He wrote a charming letter to four-year-old Hans, creating for the little boy a tale about a beautiful garden with delicious fruit and little ponies with golden bridles and silver saddles. He wrote songs for his children, including this delightful Christmas carol:

> Our little Lord, we give thee praise
>   That thou hast deigned to take our ways.
> Born of a maid a man to be,
>   And all the angels sing to thee.
>
> The eternal Father's Son he lay
>   Cradled in a crib of hay.
> The everlasting God appears
>   In our frail flesh and blood and tears.
>
> What the globe could not enwrap
>   Nestled lies in Mary's lap.
> Just a baby, very wee,
>   Yet Lord of all the world is he.

Luther could be cranky with his children and occasionally severe, but he loved them deeply and was quick to learn important spiritual lessons from them. When little Martin was nursing, Luther said, 'The pope, the bishops, Duke George, Ferdinand, and all the demons hate this child, yet he isn't afraid of all of them put together.' When four-year-old Anastasia was prattling about Christ, angels, and heaven, Luther said, 'My dear child, if only we could hold fast to this faith.' 'Why, Papa,' she said, 'don't you believe it?' Luther commented: 'Christ has made the children our teachers. I am chagrined that although I am ever so much a doctor, I still have to go to the same school with Hans and Magdalena, for who among men can understand the full meaning of this word of God, "Our Father who art in heaven"?'

Luther not only learned from his children. He also learned spiritual lessons from his dog, Töpel. At mealtimes Töpel hoped for a morsel from his master, watching with open mouth and expectant eyes. Luther said, 'Oh, if I could only pray the way this dog watches the meat! All his thoughts are concentrated on the piece of meat. Otherwise he has no thought, wish, or hope.'

Martin and Katie brought up four orphaned children in addition to their own six. They took in the sick and opened their spare rooms to student boarders. The household at times numbered as many as twenty-five. Large gatherings for meals were supervised ably by Katie, with Luther holding forth on all kinds of topics, and at least one person writing it all down.

'God has taken my salvation out of my hands into his.'

While Luther was getting accustomed to married life ('One wakes up in the morning,' Luther said, 'and finds a pair of pigtails on the pillow which were not there before'), he was also working on a book, *On the Bondage of the Will*, his answer to *On Free Will* by Erasmus. Luther's book was a major accomplishment (he thought so himself!) in which he defended what he now saw as the teaching of St Paul, as well as St Augustine, that God's salvation was an absolutely free gift to undeserving sinners. Oberman wisely comments that Luther's *Bondage of the Will* could much better have been called *The Majesty of God*, which would immediately have revealed what was at stake.[12] Along with his biblical and theological arguments, Luther includes words of his own personal testimony. He wrote: 'For my own part, I frankly confess that even if it were possible, I should not wish to have free choice given to me, or to have anything left in my own hands by which I might strive toward salvation. For, on the one hand, I should be unable to stand firm and keep hold of it amid so many adversities and perils and so many assaults of demons, seeing that even one demon is mightier than all men, and no man at all could be saved; and on the other hand, even if there were no perils or adversities or demons, I should nevertheless have to labour under perpetual uncertainty and to fight as one beating the air, since even if I lived and worked to eternity, my conscience would never be assured and certain how much it ought to do to satisfy God. For whatever work might be accomplished, there would always remain an anxious doubt whether it pleased God or whether he required something more, as the experience of all self-justifiers proves, and as I myself learned to my bitter cost through so many years. But now, since God has taken my salvation out of my hands into his, making it depend on his choice and not mine, and has promised to save me, not by my own work or exertion but by his grace and mercy, I am assured and certain both that he is faithful and will not lie to me, and also that he is too great and powerful for any demons or any adversities to be able to break him or to snatch me from him.'

'A mighty fortress is our God.'

Luther suffered from episodes of physical illness and mental and spiritual depression, the worst coming in the summer of 1527. He described it in a letter to Melanchthon. 'I spent more than a week in death and in hell. My entire body was in pain, and I still tremble. Completely abandoned by Christ, I laboured under the vacillations and storms of desperation and blasphemy against God. But through the prayers of the saints God began to have mercy on me and pulled my soul from the inferno below.' Then Luther wrote his greatest hymn, 'A Mighty Fortress is Our God', based on Psalm 46. Roland Bainton claims that in this hymn, 'more than elsewhere, we have the epitome of Luther's religious character'.[13]

> A mighty fortress is our God,
> A bulwark never failing;
> Our helper he amid the flood
> Of mortal ills prevailing.
> For still our ancient foe
> Doth seek to work us woe;

    His craft and pow'r are great;
      And armed with cruel hate,
  On earth is not his equal.

Did we in our own strength confide,
  Our striving would be losing;
Were not the right man on our side,
  The man of God's own choosing.
    Dost ask who that may be?
    Christ Jesus, it is he,
    Lord Sabaoth his name,
    From age to age the same,
And he must win the battle.

And though this world, with devils filled,
  Should threaten to undo us,
We will not fear, for God has willed
  His truth to triumph through us.
    The prince of darkness grim,
    We tremble not for him;
    His rage we can endure,
    For lo! his doom is sure;
One little word shall fell him.

That word above all earthly pow'rs,
  No thanks to them, abideth;
The Spirit and the gifts are ours
  Through him who with us sideth.
    Let goods and kindred go,
    This mortal life also;

> The body they may kill:
> God's truth abideth still;
> His kingdom is forever.

Luther said: 'We sing this psalm to the praise of God, because God is with us and powerfully and miraculously preserves and defends his church and his word against all fanatical spirits, against the implacable hatred of the devil, and against all the assaults of the world, the flesh, and sin.'

'The prince of darkness grim,
we tremble not for him.'

The devil was very real to Luther—and very powerful. Luther said, 'The devil is as big as the world, as wide as the world, and he extends from heaven down into hell.' Luther wrote in the preface to his Latin works, 'Reader, be commended to God, and pray for the increase of preaching against Satan. For he is powerful and wicked, today and more dangerous than ever before, because he knows that he has only a short time left to rage.'

Luther sometimes dealt with the devil by making fun of him with coarse, rude language. He found ways to answer the devil's theological arguments. Luther told a guest who was obsessed by thoughts of his sins: 'Do not argue with Satan about the law. Make him discuss grace.' At table one day he said, 'When Satan leads me to the law I am damned, but if I can take hold of the promise I am free.' 'Almost every night when I wake up the devil is there and wants to dispute with me,' Luther said. 'No man should be alone when he opposes Satan. The church and the ministry of the word were instituted for this purpose, that hands may be joined together and one may help another.'

In 1527 or 1528 Luther wrote a personal confession of faith that was, he believed, what 'all true Christians believe' and what 'the Holy Scriptures teach us'. He added: 'I pray that all godly hearts will bear me witness of this, and pray for me that I may persevere firmly in this faith to the end of my life. For if in the assault of temptation or the pangs of death I should say something different—which God forbid—let it be disregarded; for I declare publicly that it would be incorrect, and spoken under the devil's influence. In this may my Lord and Saviour Jesus Christ assist me: blessed be he for ever. Amen.'

'This is by no means our cause.'

The Diet of Augsburg met during the summer of 1530. It was an important confrontation between the Roman Catholic and Lutheran parties in the presence of Emperor Charles V. Martin Luther, still under the ban of the empire, could not attend. He got as close as he safely could at the Castle Coburg, within the borders of Electoral Saxony. For six months he was again 'in the wilderness', as he had been at the Wartburg. There was little he could do but read, think, write, pray, and worry.

On the walls of the room he used as a study he wrote the words of Psalm 118:17, 'I shall not die, but I shall live and recount the deeds of the LORD.' He encouraged himself with the thought that 'though the cause be great, he who has brought it about, who directs and guides it, is great too, yes, the Almighty Creator of heaven and earth. This is by no means our cause, so why should we keep on tormenting ourselves over it or plaguing ourselves to death?'

Luther worried that Melanchthon, speaking for the Lutherans at the Diet, would yield too much to the Roman Catholics, but in the end he was immensely pleased with the Augsburg Confession, even approving its moderate tone as better than anything he could have written.

News of his father's death reached Luther at Coburg. He took his Psalter, went to his room, and wept for two days. He had written his father a warm letter in which he urged him to lean on 'that certain, true helper, Jesus Christ, the one who has gobbled up death and sin for our sakes'. 'My father,' Luther wrote, 'fell asleep softly and strong in the faith in Christ.' The following year Luther's mother died.

'Faith gives joy, comfort, and peace.'

A seal for Martin Luther was designed at the behest of John Frederick of Saxony in 1530, while Luther was at the Coburg Castle. Luther saw it as a 'symbol of his theology'. In a letter of July 8, 1530, he explained its meaning:

'There is a black cross in a heart which retains its natural colour of red, so that I myself would be reminded that faith in the Crucified saves us. "For one who believes from the heart will be justified." Although it is indeed a black cross, which mortifies and causes pain, it leaves the heart in its natural colour. It does not corrupt nature, that is, it does not kill but keeps alive. "The just shall live by faith."

'Such a heart stands in the middle of a white rose, to show that faith gives joy, comfort, and peace.

'Such a rose stands in a sky-blue field, symbolizing that such joy in spirit and faith is a beginning of the heavenly future joy, which begins already, but is grasped in hope, not yet revealed.

'And around this field is a golden ring, symbolizing that such blessedness in heaven lasts forever and has no end. Such blessedness is exquisite, beyond all joy and goods, just as gold is the most valuable, most precious, and best metal.'

'The theology in the 127 volumes [of Luther's works],' writes Martin E. Marty, 'is in a way a set of footnotes to the seal.'[14] The seal is also a summary of Luther's testimony—in colour.

'The years are piling up.'

Martin Luther was thirty-four years old when he wrote the Ninety-five Theses. He was thirty-seven when he was excommunicated by the Roman Catholic Church, forty-one when he married Katharina von Bora, and forty-six when the Augsburg Confession was produced in 1530. That event marks 'a plausible dividing line between the younger and the older Luther', writes Mark Edwards.[15]

Luther was still a middle-aged man, but he felt old. 'The years are piling up,' he lamented. He was experiencing episodes of alarming, painful illness. In March 1531, he wrote, 'I am seriously declining in strength, especially in the head. It hinders me from writing, reading, or speaking much, and I am living like a sick man.' The next year he had to give up preaching for a time because dizziness made it impossible for him to complete a sermon. He struggled with deep depression. 'I can't banish the thought from my mind,' he said, 'when I wish that I had never started [the reform of the church]. So likewise when I wish I were dead rather than witness such contempt [for the word of God and his faithful servants].'

According to Roland Bainton, Martin Luther became 'prematurely an irascible old man, petulant, peevish, unrestrained, and at times positively coarse'. But, writes Bainton, 'Luther's later years are ... by no means to be written off as the sputterings of a dying flame.'[16] Oberman notes that 'Luther's recollections [in the *Table Talk*] do not have the function of self-glorification, nor do they look back to the "good old days" of a man who is getting on in years.'[17]

Despite advancing age, chronic illness, and debilitating depression, Luther gave himself to the preservation of the church that he had done so much to create and define. Martin Brecht writes in the foreword to the third volume of his Luther biography, 'The subtitle of this volume indicates what was most important for the old Luther: the preservation of the church.' Acknowledging Luther's bitterness to his enemies, rudeness to his friends, and 'serious errors both in practice and in theory', Brecht concludes that 'to the end, however, his positive contributions and deep insights remained more significant. Abruptness and resignation were not able to stifle the tender tones and the fundamental trust in God that came from his belief in justification by faith.'[18]

Luther wrote in his *Address to the Christian Nobility* that Christ seeks as his representatives on earth not popes and prelates but ministers in the form of servants, the form in which he went about on earth 'working, preaching, suffering, and dying'. 'Neither sweat nor sword can ever advance the messianic kingdom,' said Luther. Rather it comes by 'enduring, working, persevering, waiting—publicly proclaiming the gospel, openly beseeching God to intervene'.

'There is nothing I want more than to make God's gospel known.'

Much of Luther's time in his later years was spent preaching and teaching—'allowing the Scriptures of the past to become the tidings of the present,' writes Oberman.[19] 'There is nothing I want more,' said Luther, 'than to make God's gospel known to the world and to convert many people.'

Luther taught his students at the University of Wittenberg. His teaching is illustrated by his *Lectures on Genesis*, delivered from 1535 to 1545. He went far beyond the actual text, leaving very few theological problems and issues untouched. In these lectures we find, writes Heiko Oberman, 'concentrated summaries of his theology'.[20] Luther told his students that 'Genesis is a charming book and has wonderful stories. I can't altogether understand it, however. I'll have to be dead four years or so before I comprehend fully what creation means and what the omnipotence of God is.' Luther was not satisfied with his work. 'The lectures are hastily thrown together and are imperfect,' he said. 'I can't do justice to such a thing while I'm busy with many tasks. To do much and to do it well don't fit together.'

Luther was glad to be a preacher. 'If I could today become king or emperor, I would not give up my office as preacher,' he said. He preached frequently at the city church in Wittenberg, faithfully carrying on his ministry during times of pestilence when some sought safer places. Luther said, 'It pleases me very much that the Jews apply Psalm 91, "He who dwells in the shadow of the Most High", to the pestilence.'

Late in 1536 Luther said, 'I've preached here [in the city church of Wittenberg] for twenty-four years. I've walked to church so often that it wouldn't be at all surprising if I had not only worn out my shoes on the pavement but even my feet.' 'When I preach here,' he told a visiting pastor, 'I adapt myself to the circumstances of the common people. I don't look at the doctors and masters, of whom scarcely forty are present, but at the hundred or the thousand young people and children. It's to them that I preach, to them that I devote myself, for they, too, need to understand. If the others don't want to listen they can leave.'

Luther loved preaching, and he knew its challenges and hardships. 'If I were to write about the burdens of the preacher as I have experienced them and as I know them,' Luther said, 'I would scare everybody off.' He wrote, 'Our Lord God had to ask Moses as many as six times. He also led me into the office [of preacher] in the same way. Had I known about it beforehand, he would have had to take more pains to get me in.' 'I have never been troubled by my inability to preach well,' Luther made clear, 'but I have often been alarmed and frightened to think that I was obliged to speak thus in God's presence about his mighty majesty and divine nature.'

Luther also knew the power of preaching. 'God says to us, "Preach! I shall give the increase. I know the hearts of men." This should be our comfort, even when the world laughs at our office.' Luther preached, and he preached to the very end. His last sermon was given on February 15, 1546, three days before his death. The location of his grave, chosen with great care, was near the pulpit in the Castle Church of Wittenberg.

'Dear Master Peter ... '

Luther wrote hundreds of letters during his later years in which he offered instruction, counsel, comfort, correction, and warning. He produced pastoral writings to deal with the problems and questions people faced.

He wrote a charming little book for his friend and barber, Peter Beskendorf, who asked Luther one day for instruction on how to pray. In it Luther speaks 'as simply as he could on the most profound issue he knew'.[21] 'Dear Master Peter,' he wrote: 'I will tell you as best I can what I do personally when I pray. May our dear Lord grant to you and to every-body to do it better than I!'

'Many times I have learned more from one prayer than I might have learned from much reading and speculation.'

'When I feel that I have become cool and joyless in prayer because of other tasks or thoughts (for the flesh and the devil always impede and obstruct prayer), I take my little Psalter, hurry to my room, or if it be the day and hour for it, to the church where a congregation is assembled, and, as time permits, I say quietly to myself and word-for-word the Ten Commandments, the Creed, and, if I have time, some words of Christ or of Paul, or some psalms, just as a child might do.'

He described the way he used the Lord's Prayer: 'To this day I suckle at the Lord's Prayer like a child, and as an old man eat and drink from it and never get my fill. It is the very best prayer, even better than the Psalter, which is so very dear to me. It is surely evident that a real Master composed and taught it.'

Luther's *Comfort for Women Who Have Had a Miscarriage* grew out of his concern that mothers whose babies die before or at birth know that God is not angry with them, that his 'will is always better than ours, though it may seem otherwise to us from our human point of view'. Babies, though unbaptized, are not lost, Luther wrote, but saved by the prayers of their parents 'in view of the promise that God willed to be their God'.

A man kept asking Luther for help with his fear of death. Although extremely busy, Luther found time to produce a treatise, called *A Sermon on Preparing to Die*, with twenty points!

'Music is a gift of God.'

The Bible, the catechism, the liturgy, and the hymnbook—the needs of the Protestant Church—were all met by Luther himself. He emphasized congregational singing to encourage lay participation in worship and to teach true doctrine to ordinary people. His love for music—he said that 'music is an endowment and a gift of God', second only to theology as a comfort to the human soul—and the hymns he wrote, with those he inspired, established his reputation as 'father of the German hymn'.[22]

Luther's hymns were often statements of his testimony.

> Forlorn and lost in death I lay,
>   A captive of the devil,
> My sin lay heavy, night and day,
>   For I was born in evil.
>   I fell but deeper for my strife,
>   There was no good in all my life,
>   For sin had all possessed me.
>
> My good works they were worthless quite,
>   A mock was all my merit;
> My will hated God's judging light,
>   To all good dead and buried.
>   E'en to despair me anguish bore,
>   That nought but death lay me before;
>   To hell I fast was sinking.
>
> Then God was sorry on his throne
>   To see such torment rend me;
> His tender mercy he thought on,
>   His good help he would send me.
>   He turned to me his father-heart;
>   Ah! then was his no easy part,
>   For of his best it cost him.

'For of his best it cost him.' God's grace in Christ is the theme of Luther's hymns, his theology, and his testimony. On one occasion, during family devotions, Luther told the story of God's commanding Abraham to sacrifice his son Isaac. When he finished, Katie said, 'I don't believe it.

God would not have treated his son like that.' 'But, Katie,' answered Luther, 'he did.'

'I must root out the stumps and bushes.'

In his last years Luther produced a stream of polemical writings against a variety of foes—Roman Catholics (including Erasmus), other Protestants (including renegade Lutherans, Zwinglians, and Anabaptists), Turks, and Jews. These writings, according to the *Oxford Dictionary of the Christian Church*, 'are prone to frequent lapses into personal abuse of his opponents'.

Luther believed that his polemical writings were necessary. When asked why he wrote with such vehemence, he answered, 'I was born to go to war and give battle to sects and devils. That is why my books are stormy and warlike. I must root out the stumps and bushes and hack away the thorns and brambles. I am the great lumberjack who must clear the land and level it.' Melanchthon agreed. He said in his funeral oration for his friend, 'God gave this last age a sharp physician on account of its great sickness.'

Luther knew that anger was his besetting sin. At times he was 'proud and arrogant—as you see in my books that I despise my adversaries. I take them for fools.' 'Wrath just will not let go of me,' he wrote. 'Why, sometimes I rage about a silly little thing not worth mentioning. Whoever crosses my path has to pay for it, and I won't say a kind word to anyone.' Some felt that Luther went much too far in his denunciation of others. Even Katie objected. Luther was harshly criticizing Caspar Schwenckfeld's book, when Katie interrupted, 'Ah, dear sir, that's much too coarse!' Luther replied that people like Schwenckfeld caused him to be coarse, because 'this is the way one must talk to the devil'.

Most of Luther's polemical writings were directed against Roman Catholic opponents. In January of 1546, a few weeks before he died, he began a treatise against the Louvain theologians. He was more enraged at them than befits a theologian and an old man, Luther explained, 'but one must resist Satan's monsters even if one must blow at them with one's last breath!' Luther's attacks on fellow Protestants were almost as sharp. He wrote against the Turks, and much more bitterly against the Jews.

In 1541 Elector John Frederick asked Luther to write an appeal for prayer against the Turks to help build morale for defeating the Turks militarily. But in his *Appeal* Luther seemed more concerned with the lack of Christian commitment on the part of the German people. He saw the advancing Turkish armies as a sign of God's rod of chastisement: 'They say there is no helping up a man who turns down good counsel. We Germans have heard the word of God now for many years, by which God, the Father of all mercies, enlightens us and calls us from the abominable darkness and idolatry of the papacy into the light of his holy kingdom. But today it is a horrible sight to see how thankless and ungrateful we have been toward it.'

Luther concluded his appeal by warning that 'we Christians are not to put our hope in our cleverness, nor in our might. Our solace, boldness, self-confidence, security, victory, life, joy, our honour and glory are seated up there in person at the right hand of God the Father Almighty. We commit all to him. He will do all things well as he has from the beginning, does now, and always will do unto all eternity. Amen.'

Martin Luther's writings about the Jews shifted from cautious optimism to harsh denunciation. The young Luther was known as a friend of the Jews. He boldly stated that 'Jesus Christ was born a Jew', that the Jews are God's people, and that we Gentiles are only 'in-laws and aliens'. He believed that if the Jews were treated kindly and correctly taught the Holy Scripture, many of them would become true Christians and would return to the faith of their fathers, the prophets and the patriarchs. Luther did not charge the Jews with being 'Christ killers'. A hymn ascribed to him, published at Wittenberg in 1544, has the words:

> 'Twas our great sins and misdeeds gross
> Nailed Jesus, God's true Son, to the cross.
> Thus you, poor Judas, we dare not blame,
> Nor the band of Jews; ours is the shame.

When Jews converted to Christianity, Luther believed, they became full brothers and sisters in Christ, but few Jews became Christians. He was disappointed and angry. He wrote a book called *Of the Jews and Their Lies*, in which he urged German leaders to 'chase all the Jews out of their land'. It was, writes Eric Gritsch, 'an unforgivably harsh judgment' for one who had shown so much love for the people of Israel in his work as an Old Testament scholar.[23]

'I almost talked the whole world to death.'

In March 1545 Luther completed the preface to the Wittenberg edition of his Latin writings. At times he seemed proud and pleased that he had written so many books. At other times he expressed misgivings about them. When friends were urging Luther to allow them to publish his collected works, he said, 'I wished that all my books were buried in perpetual oblivion, so that there might be room for better ones.' When he completed his large commentary on Galatians, he said, 'I wonder who encourages this mania for writing! Who wants to buy such stout tomes? And if they're bought, who'll read them? And if they're read, who'll be edified by them?' Luther said that he didn't like his commentary on the Psalms, because it contained 'a great deal of idle chatter. I used to be so fluent that I almost talked the whole world to death.' Later Luther said, 'If my advice were taken, only the books of mine that contain doctrine would be printed, such as my Galatians, Deuteronomy, and John. The rest of my books should be read merely for the history, in order to see how it all began.'

'We just have to patch and darn as best we can.'

Luther spent the last years of his life attempting to support the religious movement he began and to prevent it from becoming entangled with political interests. He did not relish this role. Others are 'more learned than I am in economic and political matters,' Luther said. 'I'm not interested in such things. I'm concerned about the church and must defend myself against the attacks of the devil.'

Luther had no great hope for much improvement in the state of the world. He said, 'God does not think so much of his temporal realm as he does of his spiritual realm. So I would not advise that any changes be made. We just have to patch and darn as best we can while we live, punish the abuses, and lay bandages and poultices over the sores.' Luther's illustration of the futility of political efforts to solve the world's problems is often quoted: 'The world is like a drunken peasant. If you lift him into the saddle on one side, he will fall off on the other side. One can't help him, no matter how one tries. He wants to be the devil's.'

Despite these pessimistic statements, Luther did not give way to cynicism or passivity. He tried to help make life in this world more tolerable. The last days of his life were spent at the negotiating table dealing with a secular matter. Years earlier in his *Address to the Christian Nobility* Luther had written to German leaders that they should work for 'repentance, repair, and reform [but] with no prospect of a golden age until after the Second Coming'. Luther looked forward to that day when all would be made right. 'I think the last day is not far off,' he commented at table. 'My reason is that a last great effort is now being made to advance the gospel. It's like a candle. Just before it burns out it makes a last great spurt, as if it would continue to burn for a long time, and then it goes out.'

'My times are in your hand.'

During the last decade and a half of his life Luther's physical ailments and discomforts were critical and at times life threatening. He was often in pain, sometimes in agony, from kidney and gall stones, stomach disorders, increasing deafness, shortness of breath, severe headaches, and heart problems. He suffered mentally and emotionally, troubled by spiritual depression and despair for the world, and sometimes for the church. He was deeply disappointed about the lack of progress in the Reformation movement and anxious about the dangers that political involvement might bring. Luther confessed that 'nothing has so exhausted me as sorrow, especially at night'. Toward the end he began to question his own sanity. 'Well. All right,' Luther decided. 'If I go mad, God will remain sane and Christ my Lord will be my wisdom.'

Luther said we must 'double up our fists and pray', but he admitted that it was not always easy to do so. He sought help from others. Luther recalled that in one of his dark times John Bugenhagen said to him, 'God must surely be asking himself, "What can I still make of this man? I have given him so many superb gifts, but now he questions my grace."' 'For me,' Luther said, 'this was an immense comfort, like the sound of angels echoing in my heart.'

In times of depression, Luther also depended on Katie's love and wisdom. Eating a favourite meal (Luther loved fried herring with mustard and cold peas) and drinking good beer also helped. Music, he found, was a good way to 'banish trials and thoughts', since the devil hates it so.

Above all, Luther turned to the Bible in times of trouble. Preaching from 1 Peter 5:5-11, he urged Christians to fling aside 'care and fearful apprehensions but not into a corner, for when cares cling to the heart, they cannot be flung aside in that way. Let the Christian learn to cast both his heart and his cares upon God's back, for God has a strong neck and strong shoulders; he can easily carry the load.'

Commenting on Ecclesiastes 6:12, Luther asked, 'Why are we so vexed by thoughts, seeing that the future is not in our power for one moment? Let us, then, be satisfied with the present and commit ourselves to the hand of God, who alone knows and controls the past and the future.'

He found help in Psalm 31, admitting that he had not really understood 'My times are in your hand' until then. 'That is, my whole life, each day, hour, moment—which is the same as to say, "My health, sickness, misfortune, happiness, life, death, joy, and sorrow are in your hand."' Luther believed that affliction teaches one 'to experience how right, how true, how sweet, how lovely, how comforting God's word is, wisdom beyond all wisdom'. 'Affliction,' Luther said, 'is the best book in my library.'

'Dear Magdalena, my little daughter.'

Nothing caused Luther greater suffering than the death of his thirteen-year-old daughter, Magdalena, on September 20, 1542.[24] Luther said to her, 'Dear Magdalena, my little daughter, you would be glad to stay here with me, your father. Are you also glad to go to your Father in heaven?' She answered, 'Yes, dear father, as God wills.'

The separation caused by her death troubled him above measure. He said, 'It's strange to know that she is surely at peace and that she is well off with her Father in heaven, very well off, and yet to grieve so much!' When Magdalena's body was placed in a coffin, Luther looked at her and said, 'Ah, dear child, to think that you must be raised up and will shine like the stars, yes, like the sun!' When she was buried, Luther comforted himself, affirming that 'there is a resurrection of the flesh'.

Luther composed the epitaph for Magdalena:

> I, Lena, Luther's beloved child
>> Sleep gently here with all the saints
> And lie at peace and rest
>> Now I am our God's own guest.

I was a child of death, it is true,
My mother bore me out of mortal seed,
Now I live and am rich in God.
For this I thank Christ's death and blood.

'I am dying but God lives.'

Luther greeted the new year of 1538 with the words, 'How good, joyful, and auspicious is the beginning of a new year for the glory of Christ, the salvation of his church, and the confusion of Satan and his adherents!' He revelled in the flowers of a spring day, 'whose blooms are a parable of the resurrection of the dead. How pleasant the trees are! How delightfully green everything is beginning to be! If God can take such delight in our earthly sojourn, what must it be like in the life to come?'

But more and more Luther found living in this world a disappointment and trial and looked forward to its end. He declared, 'I am quite tired of living. May our Lord God come soon and quickly take me away!' He said, 'I am now exhausted and full of cares, yet I am plagued with many duties.' A few years later he confessed, 'I'm fed up with the world, and it is fed up with me.'

Luther said: 'Long enough now have I played this game against the pope and the devil, and the Lord has wonderfully protected and comforted me. Why shouldn't I now bear with equanimity what he does with me according to his will? In any case our death is nothing compared with the death of the Son of God. Besides, so many very saintly men have been buried before us whose company we are not worthy of; if we desire to be with them, as we really do desire, it's necessary that we die. We ought to reach out for this with an eager spirit because our Lord is the Lord of life who holds us in his hand.'

In his ten-year-long course of lectures on the book of Genesis, Luther came to the last chapters as he came to the last weeks of his life. There he found much to strengthen his own faith. He said about Jacob's death, 'Jacob dies, it is true, yet his death is tantamount to life—indeed, it is the closest thing to life.' Luther spoke for Jacob in the first person, 'I am dying and shall lie in the sepulchre, but God lives. He who has promised the land into which he will lead you will also set me over into another, far better land. For it is his promise.' Luther lectured for a few more weeks on the burial of Jacob and on Joseph's death and burial, and finally ended his labour on the book of Genesis with the words, 'And that is the sweet book of Genesis. May our Lord God give it to others to do a better job after me. I can do no more. I am weak. Pray God for me, that he may give me a blissful end.'

On February 7, 1546, in a playful and bantering tone, Luther wrote to his wife from Eisleben where he had made a third trip to help two counts, who were brothers, reconcile their differences:

'To my dear wife, Katharina Luther, doctoress and self-tormentor at Wittenberg, my gracious lady,

'Grace and peace in the Lord! Read, dear Katie, the Gospel of John and the Small Catechism, of which you once said: Indeed, everything in this book is said about me. For you want to assume the cares of your God, just as if he were not almighty and were unable to create ten Dr Martins if this old one were drowned in the Saale or suffocated in a stove or trapped on Wolf's fowling floor. Leave me in peace with your worrying! I have a better Caretaker than you and all the angels. He it is who lies in a manger and nurses at a virgin's breast, but at the same time sits at the right hand of God, the almighty Father. Therefore be at rest. Amen.'

'We are beggars. That is true.'

There are many great events in Luther's life, but none greater than his last few days. The day before he died he wrote a few lines in Latin, found next to his deathbed: 'No one should believe that he has tasted the Holy Scriptures sufficiently unless he has spent one hundred years leading churches with the prophets.' This was followed by the words 'We are beggars' in German, and, in Latin, 'That is true.' With these words Luther aptly and humbly summed up his life as a Reformer and theologian. It was not what he did, but what God did for and through him that mattered.

Many years earlier Luther wrote a version of the *Nunc Dimittis*, which became his dying testimony:

> In peace and joy I now depart,
> As God wants me.

> Content and still is mind and heart,
>   He doth save me.
> As my God hath promised me,
>   Death is become my slumber.

Martin Luther died in the early morning hours of February 18, 1546, only a few steps from the house in Eisleben where he had been born sixty-two years earlier. A crowd of people surrounded his bed and heard Luther repeating again and again the words 'For God so loved the world that he gave his only Son.' Luther's one great message was that 'the life of a Christian is linked to the lifeline of mercy which God established in Christ. Thus the Christian truly lives by faith alone rather than by the merit of good works aimed at pacifying God.'[25] Luther's long-time friend, Justin Jonas, pastor in Halle, asked, 'Reverend father, will you die steadfast in Christ and the doctrines you have preached?' 'Yes,' replied the clear voice for the last time. Luther's testimony is summed up in that little word 'yes'.

At his funeral, Luther's hymn on Psalm 130 was sung. Once again people heard Luther's testimony:

> To wash away the crimson stain,
>   Grace, grace alone availeth;
> Our works, alas! are all in vain;
>   In much the best life faileth:
>   No man can glory in thy sight,
>   All must alike confess thy might,
>   And live alone by mercy.

Endnotes

[1] Heiko A. Oberman, *Luther: Man Between God and the Devil* (New York: Doubleday, 1992), 312.

[2] Luther's *Preface to His Latin Writings* is found in the *American Edition of Luther's Works* (St. Louis: Concordia; Philadelphia: Fortress Press, 1955-196), volume 34: 327-38. Martin Brecht calls Luther's preface 'an important historical personal testimony' (*Martin Luther: The Preservation of the Church 1532-1546* [Minneapolis: Fortress Press, 1993], 144). The *Table Talk* includes 6,596 entries from Luther! Many of these are found in *Luther's Works* volume 54. Many excellent biographies provide full treatment of the Reformer's life and times, such as Roland Bainton's *Here I Stand: A Life of Martin Luther* (New York: Mentor, 1950); James Kittelson's *Luther: The Reformer: The Story of the Man and His Career* (Minneapolis: Augsburg Publishing House, 1986); and Heiko A. Oberman's *Luther: Man Between God and the Devil* (New York: Doubleday, 1992).

[3] Thomas Carlyle, *Heroes and Hero-Worship* (London: James Fraser, 1841). Roland Bainton writes that Carlyle's 'sketch of Luther bristles with a vitality beyond many a learned tome'. Roland H. Bainton, *Yesterday, Today, and What Next?* (Minneapolis: Augsburg Publishing House, 1978), 11.

[4] Oberman, *Luther*, 114.

[5] Oberman, *Luther*, 149. According to Roman Catholic tradition, the Scala Sancta or Holy Stairs are the steps leading up to the praetorium of Pontius Pilate in Jerusalem on which Jesus Christ stepped on his way to trial during his Passion. The Stairs reputedly were brought to Rome by St Helena in the fourth century. For centuries, the Scala Sancta have attracted Christian pilgrims who wish to honour the Passion of Jesus Christ.

[6] Luther tells the story of how he discovered justification by faith in Romans 1 several times—in the *Preface to His Latin Writings*

(336-37) and in the *Table Talk* (193-94, 309). I have combined material from these several sources.

[7] Bainton, *Here I Stand*, 150.

[8] Bainton, *Here I Stand*, 255.

[9] H. G. Haile, *Luther: An Experiment in Biography* (New York: Doubleday, 1980), 264.

[10] Haile, *Luther*, 262.

[11] Oberman, *Luther*, 273.

[12] Oberman, *Luther*, 212.

[13] Bainton, *Here I Stand*, 270.

[14] Martin E. Marty, *October 31, 1517: Martin Luther and the Day that Changed the World* (Brewster, Mass.: Paraclete Press, 2016).

[15] Mark U. Edwards, Jr., *Luther's Last Battles: Politics and Polemics 1531-46* (Minneapolis: Fortress Press, 2005), 10.

[16] Bainton, *Here I Stand*, 292, 300.

[17] Oberman, *Luther*, 106.

[18] Brecht, *Martin Luther,* xii.

[19] Oberman, *Luther*, 173.

[20] Oberman, *Luther*, 166.

[21] Haile, *Luther*, 57.

[22] Haile, *Luther*, 53.

[23] Eric W. Gritsch, *Martin—God's Court Jester: Luther in Retrospect* (Philadelphia: Fortress Press, 1983), 83.

[24] Luther's eight-month-old daughter, Elizabeth, had died August 3, 1528.

[25] Gritsch, *Martin*, 75.

2

John Calvin's Testimony

Heiko Oberman says that Luther's personal experience is always present in his writings, but 'the personality of Calvin retreats into the background even in personal correspondence'.[1] It is true that compared with Luther, Calvin's autobiographical comments are sparse, but we do find his testimony in the preface to his *Commentary on the Psalms*, his *Reply to Sadoleto*, his letters, and occasional remarks in his sermons, commentaries and treatises.[2] To Sadoleto, Calvin wrote, 'It is true that I do not speak of myself willingly; since nevertheless I cannot be entirely silent, I will speak of myself as modestly as I can.' Even when Calvin is not speaking of himself his testimony is present in his work. Elsie McKee has written, 'Calvin's own life was so intertwined with his ministry, whether immediately in Geneva or indirectly much farther afield, that it is difficult to speak of his personal biography apart from his office.'[3]

'When I was a very little boy, my father had destined me for the study of theology.'

John Calvin was born in Noyon, France, on July 10, 1509. He was baptized a few days later in the local cathedral, where his father, Gérard, was employed by the bishop and the cathedral chapter to perform a variety of administrative functions. In his *Institutes of the Christian Religion* Calvin reflected on his own baptism, 'We indeed, being blind and unbelieving, for a long time did not grasp the promise that had been given us in baptism; yet that promise, since it was of God, ever remained fixed and firm and trustworthy.' His devout mother, Jeanne Le Franc, died when John was five or six years old. He recalled in his *Treatise Concerning Relics* that as a little boy he was taken by his mother to see and kiss a fragment of the body of St Anne during a feast in her honour. His father arranged for John to be educated with the children of the local bishop's family. Even after years in Geneva, Calvin remained a Frenchman with a love for his hometown. In 1552, hearing of the destruction of Noyon by the Spanish, he wrote sadly, 'I have outlived my country, something I could never have believed.'

Calvin wrote, 'When I was a very little boy, my father had destined me for the study of theology.' When he was eleven or twelve years old he was sent to Paris to study for his arts degree. His Latin teacher was Maturin Cordier, to whom Calvin dedicated his *Commentary on 1 Thessalonians*.

Calvin wrote: 'It was under your guidance that I entered on a course of studies, and made progress at least to the extent of being of some benefit to the church of God. When my father sent me as a boy to Paris I had done only the rudiments of Latin. For a short time, however, you were an instructor sent to me by God to teach me the true method of learning, so that I might afterwards be a little more proficient. It was my desire to testify to posterity that if they derive any profit from my writings, they should know that to some extent you are responsible for them.'

'God, by the secret guidance of his providence, gave a different direction to my course.'

'When my father,' Calvin wrote, 'considered that the legal profession commonly raised those who followed it to wealth, this prospect suddenly induced him to change his mind. Thus it came to pass, that I was withdrawn from the study of philosophy, and was put to the study of law. To this pursuit I endeavoured to apply myself, in obedience to the will of my father; but God, by the secret guidance of his providence, at length gave a different direction to my course.'

Melchior Wolmar, a law professor much influenced by Luther's views, passed on to Calvin a love for the Greek language. Calvin dedicated his *Commentary on 2 Corinthians* to his old master. He wrote: 'I remember with what affection you maintained and reinforced the beginnings of my long friendship with you; how you were ready frankly to employ yourself and your power for me when you thought the occasion presented itself for showing your love for me; how you offered your influence to advance me, if the vocation to which I was then attached had not prevented me from accepting it. But there is nothing I have found as pleasant as the remembrance of that first time, when, being sent by my father to learn civil law, I combined, having you for conductor and master, with the study of law that of Greek letters, which you were then teaching with great praise.'

Years later Calvin wrote, 'My father sent me to study law, and the death of my father [in 1531] turned me aside from that road.' Calvin's studies in law interested him, but his true passion was the humanities. He sought to establish his reputation as a scholar with his first book, a commentary on Seneca's *De clementia*, which appeared in 1532.

'God by a sudden conversion subdued and brought my mind to a teachable frame.'

In his search for salvation, Roman Catholic preaching and practice did nothing to help Calvin, but rather increased his guilt. He remembered when 'there were always those torments of conscience which made you feel as if you were in hell. I experienced it myself that way.' He wrote: 'I was God's arch-enemy, and in me there was not even a semblance of obedience toward him at all, but I was rather full of pride, full of maliciousness, arrogance and a diabolic obstinance to resist God and to plunge myself into eternal death.'

But around 1533 the brilliant young humanist, 'a lover of literature and destined for success, became a lover of Jesus Christ, eager to respond to a call'.[4] Calvin explained: 'Since I was too obstinately addicted to the superstitions of popery to be easily extricated from so profound an abyss of mire, God by a sudden conversion subdued and brought my mind to a teachable frame, which was more hardened in such matters than might have been expected from one at my early period of life.'

Scholars have attempted to discover what or who influenced Calvin in his sudden change of heart, but he simply says that God did it. Calvin's use of the word 'sudden' has received considerable attention. Does it mean 'suddenly', or does it mean 'unexpected', or should it be translated 'providential'? Perhaps the best interpretation of Calvin's word is that after a time of study and uncertainty Calvin came providentially to a clear and final decision.

Years later, writing on the sacraments, Calvin supplied a further glimpse into his experience. As he began to loosen himself from Rome, he read the writings of Luther and some other Reformers. He clearly preferred Luther. He explained: 'As I began to emerge a little from the shadows of the papacy, and having enjoyed a small taste of the pure doctrine, when I read in Luther that Oecolampadius and Zwingli left nothing of the sacraments but naked figures and symbols without reality, I confess that this turned me away from their books, so that for a long time I refrained from reading them.'[5]

'I at length perceived, as if light had broken in upon me, in what a style of error I had wallowed.'

In 1539 Calvin answered the letter that Cardinal Sadoleto had written to the Genevans inviting them to return to the Catholic faith. Calvin's reply includes the testimonies of a Protestant minister and of a layman before the judgment seat of God in answer to Sadoleto's 'fictitious one which you, in order to aggravate our case, were pleased to devise'. Calvin's words of the layman, according to John T. McNeill, were 'a more or less conscious tabulation of some of the problems that were exercising Calvin's mind before his conversion and the solutions of them found in that experience'.[6]

'I, O Lord, as I had been educated from a boy, always professed the Christian faith. But at first I had no other reason for my faith than that which then everywhere prevailed. Your word, which ought to have shone on all your people like a lamp, was taken away, or at least suppressed as to us. And lest anyone should long for greater light, an idea had been instilled into the minds of all, that the investigation of that hidden celestial philosophy was better delegated to a few, whom the others might consult as oracles—that the highest knowledge befitting plebeian minds was to subdue themselves into obedience to the Church.

Then, the rudiments in which I had been instructed were of a kind which could neither properly train me to the legitimate worship of your Deity, nor pave the way for me to a sure hope of salvation, nor train me aright for the duties of the Christian life.

'I had learned, indeed, to worship you only as my God, but as the true method of worshipping was altogether unknown to me, I stumbled at the very threshold. I believed, as I had been taught, that I was redeemed by the death of your Son from liability to eternal death, but the redemption I thought of was one whose virtue could never reach me. I anticipated a future resurrection, but hated to think of it, as being an event most dreadful. And this feeling not only had dominion over me in private, but was derived from the doctrine which was then uniformly delivered to the people by their Christian teachers. They, indeed, preached of your clemency towards men, but confined it to those who should show themselves deserving of it. They, moreover, placed this desert in the righteousness of works, so that he only was received into your favour who reconciled himself to you by works. Nor, meanwhile, did they disguise the fact, that we are miserable sinners, that we often fall through infirmity of the flesh, and that to all, your mercy behooved to be the common haven of salvation; but the method of obtaining it, which they pointed out, was by making satisfaction to you for offences. Then, the satisfaction enjoined was, first, after confessing all our sins to a priest, suppliantly to ask pardon and absolution; and secondly, by good to efface from your remembrance our bad actions. Lastly, in order to supply what was still wanting, we were to add sacrifices and solemn expiations. Then, because you were a stern judge and strict avenger of iniquity, they showed how dreadful your presence must be. Hence they bade us flee first to the saints, that by their intercession you might be rendered exorable and propitious to us.

'When, however, I had performed all these things, though I had some intervals of quiet, I was still far off from true peace of conscience; for, whenever I descended into myself, or raised my mind to you, extreme terror seized me—terror which no expiations nor satisfactions could cure. And the more closely I examined myself, the sharper the stings with which my conscience was pricked, so that the only solace which remained to me was to delude myself by obliviousness. Still, as nothing better offered, I continued the course which I had begun, when, lo, a very different form of doctrine started up, not one which led us away from the Christian profession, but one which brought it back to its fountainhead, and, as it were, clearing away the dross, restored it to its original purity. Offended by the novelty, I lent an unwilling ear, and at first, I confess, strenuously and passionately resisted; for (such is the firmness or effrontery with which it is natural to men to persist in the course which they have once undertaken) it was with the greatest difficulty I was induced to confess that I had all my life long been in ignorance and error.

'My mind being now prepared for serious attention, I at length perceived, as if light had broken in upon me, in what a style of error I had wallowed, and how much pollution and impurity I had thereby contracted. Being exceedingly alarmed at the misery into which I had fallen, and much more at that which threatened me in the view of eternal death, I, as in duty bound, made it my first business to betake myself to your way, condemning my past life, not without groans and tears. And now, O Lord, what remains to a wretch like me, but instead of defence, earnestly to supplicate you not to judge according to its deserts that fearful abandonment of your word, from which, in your wondrous goodness, you have at last delivered me.'

'God led me through different turnings and changes.'

What followed for John Calvin after his conversion was a year or two of moving about, seeking 'some secluded corner' where he could study and write. 'I was immediately inflamed with so intense a desire to make progress, that although I did not altogether leave off my studies, I yet pursued them with less ardour. I was quite surprised that before a year had elapsed, all who had a desire after purer doctrine were continually coming to me to learn, although I myself was as yet but a mere novice and tyro. Being of a disposition somewhat unpolished and bashful, which led me always to love shade and retirement, I then began to seek some secluded corner where I might be withdrawn from the public view; but so far from being able to accomplish the object of my desire, all my retreats were like public schools. In short God so led me through different turnings and changes, that he never permitted me to rest in any place, until, in spite of my natural disposition he brought me forth to public notice.'

When Protestantism in Paris provoked increasing danger to its adherents Calvin left France. He went to Basle where he wrote his *Institutes of the Christian Religion* to set forth, as he explained to the French king, the 'principal truths of the Christian religion' as held by French Protestants, in order to vindicate 'from undeserved insult my brethren whose death was precious in the sight of the Lord'. Calvin visited Ferrara, returned to Basle, went to Paris, and then set out for Strasbourg. Because of the threat of war along his route he made a very wide detour to the south through Geneva.

Calvin would not live in France again. Many years later, he wrote: 'Our common home country, which is so lovely that it attracts many foreigners even from afar, I have by now had to miss for twenty-six years. But it would in no way please or agree with me to live in a country from which God's truth, the pure teaching and the doctrine of eternal salvation, have been banished.'

In 1554 Calvin wrote to the English refugees in Zurich that there was much sorrow in being banished from one's own home country, 'yet for the children of God, who know that they are the heirs of this world, it is not so difficult to be banished. It is in fact even good for them, so that through such an experience they can train themselves in being strangers on this earth.'

'God from heaven laid his mighty hand on me.'

What happened to John Calvin in Geneva changed the course of his life. He explained: 'I had resolved to continue in the same privacy and obscurity, until at length William Farel detained me at Geneva, not so much by counsel and exhortation, as by a dreadful imprecation, which I felt to be as if God from heaven laid his mighty hand on me to arrest me. As the most direct route to Strasbourg, to which I then intended to retire, was shut up by the wars, I had resolved to pass quickly by Geneva, without staying longer than a single night in that city.

'A little before this, popery had been driven from it by the exertions of William Farel and Peter Viret; but matters were not yet brought to a settled state, and the city was divided into unholy and dangerous factions. Then an individual who now basely apostatized and returned to the papists discovered me and made me known to others. Upon this, Farel, who burned with an extraordinary zeal to advance the gospel, immediately strained every nerve to detain me. And after having learned that my heart was set upon devoting myself to private studies, for which I wished to keep myself free from other pursuits, and finding that he gained nothing by entreaties, he proceeded to utter an imprecation that God would curse my retirement, and the tranquillity of the studies which I sought, if I should withdraw and refuse to give assistance when the necessity was so urgent. By this imprecation I was so stricken with terror that I desisted from the journey which I had undertaken.'

Calvin later reflected on God's ways with him: 'When I thought things would settle down, all of a sudden I was confronted with all kinds of things I had not expected. When I thought I no longer had a place, unexpectedly a little nest was prepared for me. And all that by the hand of God who will himself take care of us if we commit ourselves to him.'

Because of his 'natural bashfulness and timidity', Calvin at first would not accept any particular office in Geneva, but finally consented to become professor of Bible. Later he was admitted to the Company of Pastors. As David was taken from the sheepfold and given a work to do, Calvin wrote, so God took him from his 'obscure and humble condition' and invested him 'with the honourable office of a preacher and minister of the gospel'. Calvin later wrote to a friend, 'I have learned from experience that we cannot see very far before us. When I promised myself an easy, tranquil life, what I least expected was at hand.' 'God,' Calvin said, 'thrust me into the game.'

'I laboured with sincerity in the work of the Lord.'

When Calvin came to Geneva, 'there was preaching and that was all. There was no Reformation. Everything was in disorder.' He worked hard to create the resources for a renewed and Reformed church—a biblical model of church polity and discipline, a form of worship with the congregational singing of Psalms, instruction for the celebration of the Lord's Supper, a confession, and a catechism for the training of children.

The ministry of Calvin and Farel in Geneva, though fruitful in many ways, was marked by fierce opposition and constant unrest and tumults. The two preachers were expelled from the city during Easter week in 1538. Calvin was both shattered and relieved. Hurt by Geneva's rejection, he concluded that he was not really fitted for the work of a pastor. He was glad to leave the city. 'I was compelled to encounter these violent tempests as part of my early training; and although I did not sink under them, yet I was not sustained by such greatness of mind, as not to rejoice more than it became me, when in consequence of certain commotions, I was banished from Geneva.'

Calvin, however, did not put all the blame on his enemies in Geneva. In a letter to Farel, six months after they were expelled, Calvin wrote that they must 'acknowledge before God and his people that it is in some measure owing to our unskillfulness, indolence, negligence and error that the church committed to our care had fallen into such a sad state of collapse'. In his answer to Sadoleto's letter, Calvin wrote that he could not claim for himself 'perspicuity, erudition, prudence, ability, not even industry' in his ministry in Geneva, but only that he 'laboured with sincerity in the work of the Lord'.

'I would prefer nothing more than peaceful, scholarly work.'

John Calvin again hoped to find the 'secluded corner' that he had been seeking before reluctantly agreeing to Farel's call to Geneva. He looked forward to the quiet life of a scholar, 'free from the burden and cares' of public ministry. 'I would prefer nothing more than peaceful, scholarly work,' he wrote, 'if only he under whose command I stand would give me the freedom for it.' He wrote to a friend in Geneva, 'After that calamity, when my ministry appeared to me to be disastrous and unprosperous, I made up my mind never again to enter upon any ecclesiastical charge whatever, unless the Lord himself, by a clear and manifest call, should summon me to it.'

Despite his sorrow over their failure in Geneva, Calvin wrote to Farel that their enemies could not denounce them 'excepting in so far as God permits' and that 'we know also the end God has in view in granting such permission. Let us humble ourselves, therefore, unless we wish to strive with God when he would humble us. Meanwhile, let us wait upon God.'

John Calvin left Geneva, but he did not forget it. He wrote: 'Although Geneva was a very troublesome province to me, the thought of deserting it never entered my mind. For I considered myself placed in that position by God, like a sentry at his post from which it would be impiety on my part were I to move a single step. Yet I think you would hardly believe me were I to relate for you even a small part of those annoyances, nay miseries, which we had to endure for a whole year. This I can truly testify, that not a day passed in which I did not long for death ten times over. But as for leaving that Church to remove elsewhere, such a thought never came to my mind.'

'That most excellent servant of Christ, Martin Bucer, drew me back to a new station.'

When Calvin was 'set at liberty and loosed from the tie' of Geneva, he resolved again to 'live in a private station, free from the burden and cares of any public charge'. While he brooded over his failure in Geneva and faced an uncertain future, Martin Bucer, leader of the Reformation movement in Strasbourg, was seeking a pastor for the French-speaking refugee community in his city. Calvin wrote, 'That most excellent servant of Christ, Martin Bucer, employing a similar kind of remonstrance and protestation as that to which Farel had recourse before, drew me back to a new station.' Alarmed by the example of Jonah that Bucer set before him, Calvin gave in and went to work in Strasbourg. He was warmly welcomed, befriended, and advised by Bucer, who was eighteen years his senior and a true father-figure.

John Calvin was again a pastor. He preached, developed a Sunday liturgy and Psalter, and visited his congregation. He cared for the sick, dying, and bereaved. He invited a group of students to live in his house and met with them for instruction and prayer. And somehow he found time to write—producing a second, expanded edition of the *Institutes*, the first French edition of the same book, and a *Commentary on Romans*. In a letter to Farel, Calvin described his day: he had about twenty pages of his revised *Institutes* to prepare for the printer. Then he had to lecture and preach, write four letters, make peace between some persons who had quarrelled with each other, and 'reply to more than ten interruptions in the meantime'.

'I greet thee, who my sure Redeemer art.'

The hymn 'I Greet Thee, Who My Sure Redeemer Art' has long been connected to John Calvin. It appeared in the 1545 Strasbourg Psalter and again in the Genevan Psalter of 1551. While it is by no means certain that Calvin wrote the hymn, it beautifully expresses his theology and spirit. It can be read as part of his testimony.

> I greet thee, who my sure Redeemer art,
>   My only trust and Saviour of my heart,
> Who pain didst undergo for my poor sake:
>   I pray thee from our hearts all cares to take.

Thou art the King of mercy and of grace,
  Reigning omnipotent in every place:
So come, O King, and our whole being sway;
  Shine on us with the light of thy pure day.

Thou art the Life, by which alone we live,
  And all our substance and our strength receive;
O comfort us in death's approaching hour,
  Strong-hearted then to face it by thy power.

Thou hast the true and perfect gentleness,
  No harshness hast thou, and no bitterness;
O grant to us the grace we find in thee,
  That we may dwell in perfect unity.

Our hope is in no other save in thee;
  Our faith is built upon thy promise free;
Come, give us peace, make us so strong and sure,
  That we may conquerors be, and ills endure.

'My wife is in my thoughts day and night.'

In Strasbourg Calvin was busy, and he was also happy. Soon he would be even happier. He wrote to Farel that he was looking for a wife: 'Always keep in mind what I seek to find in her; for I am not one of those insane lovers who embrace even the vices of those they are in love with, when they are smitten at first sight with a fine figure. The only beauty which allures me is this—that she be chaste, not too nice or fastidious, economical, patient, and likely to take care of my health.'

Calvin's words, while listing some sensible requirements in a wife, seem somewhat cold and calculating. Not surprisingly several clumsy attempts failed. Calvin informed Farel, 'I have still not found a wife, and I doubt that I shall look for one any more.' But then Calvin found and married Idelette de Bure, a widow with two children. Calvin's wife was 'actually pretty', Farel noted incredulously. Calvin deeply loved his wife. When he was away from home in March 1541 the plague broke out in Strasbourg. Idelette and her two children sought safety with a brother who lived outside the city. Calvin missed her terribly and expressed his anguish in a letter to a friend. 'My wife is in my thoughts day and night.'

When their son Jacques lived only a few days, Calvin wrote: 'The Lord has certainly inflicted on us a grave and painful wound in the death of our beloved son. But he is our Father, and knows best what is good for his children.'

Idelette died in the ninth year of their marriage. Brokenhearted, Calvin wrote to Pierre Viret: 'Although the death of my wife has been exceedingly painful to me, yet I subdue my grief as well as I can. Friends, also, are earnest in their duty to me. It might be wished, indeed, that they could profit me and themselves more; yet one can scarcely say how much I am supported by their attentions. You know well how tender, or rather soft, my mind is. Had not a powerful self-control, therefore, been vouchsafed to me, I could not have borne up so long. And truly mine is no common source of grief. I have been bereaved of the best companion of my life, of the one who, had it been so ordered, would not only have been the willing sharer of my indigence, but even of my death. During her life she was the faithful helper of my ministry. From her I never experienced the slightest hindrance. She was never troublesome to me throughout the entire course of her illness; she was more anxious about her children than about herself. As I feared these private cares might annoy her to no purpose, I took occasion, on the third day before her death, to mention that I would not fail in discharging my duty to her children. Taking up the matter immediately, she said, "I have already committed them to God." When I said that that was not to prevent me from caring for them, she replied, "I know you will not neglect what you know has been committed to God.'"

A few days later Calvin wrote to Farel: 'About the sixth hour of the day, on which she yielded up her soul to the Lord, she spoke aloud, so that all saw that her heart was raised far above the world. For these were her words: "O glorious resurrection! O God of Abraham and of all our fathers, in you have the faithful trusted during so many past ages, and none of them have trusted in vain. I also will hope." May the Lord Jesus strengthen you by his Spirit; and may he support me also under this heavy affliction, which would certainly have overcome me, had not he, who raises up the prostrate, strengthens the weak, and refreshes the weary, stretched forth his hand from heaven to me.'

'I am no more than half a man,' Calvin said, 'since God recently took my wife home to himself.' Years later he wrote to console a pastor whose wife had just died: 'How deep a wound the death of your wife must have inflicted on your heart, I judge from my own feelings. For I recollect how difficult it was for me seven years ago to get over a similar sorrow.'

Calvin did not remarry. He said in a sermon: 'I do not want it attributed to me as a virtue that I am not married. I refrain from it only so as to be more free to serve God. And this is not because I think myself more virtuous than my brothers.'

'When I remember that I am not my own, I offer up my heart, presented as a sacrifice to the Lord.'

Though happy and successful in Strasbourg, John Calvin could not forget Geneva. Once his anger had cooled, he described the still-painful experience calmly and thoughtfully. He wrote to his 'beloved brethren in our Lord who are the remnant of the dispersal of the church of Geneva', encouraging them to remember that the Lord does all things 'according to the counsel of his own will' and even acts 'through the unrighteous'. He advised them to maintain the unity of the church despite their 'differences and disputes with the ministers who have succeeded us'. He urged them to 'behave like Christians' and 'concern yourselves more with what you owe to others than with what others owe to you'.

When the Genevan leaders asked Calvin to answer a letter from Cardinal Sadoleto urging them to return to the Roman Catholic fold, Calvin accepted the task. Bernard Cottret writes, 'Nothing better demonstrates the interest Calvin continued to take in Genevan affairs than his magnificent Letter to Sadoleto.'[7] Calvin explained that, although he was at present 'relieved of the charge of the Church of Geneva', he still embraced it 'with paternal affection', since God when he gave it to him 'bound me to be faithful to it forever'. Therefore, wrote Calvin, 'I cannot cast off that charge any more than that of my own soul.'

Calvin felt bound to the church in Geneva, but still he did not want to go back there. He wrote: 'When the Lord having compassion on this city had allayed the hurtful agitations and broils which prevailed in it, and by his wonderful power had defeated both the wicked counsels and the sanguinary attempts of the disturbers of the Republic, necessity was imposed upon me of returning to my former charge, contrary to my desire and inclination. The welfare of this church, it is true, lay so near my heart, that for its sake I would not have hesitated to lay down my life; but my timidity nevertheless suggested to me many reasons for excusing myself from again willingly taking upon my shoulders so heavy a burden. At length, however, a solemn and conscientious regard to my duty prevailed with me to consent to return to the flock from which I had been torn; but with what grief, tears, great anxiety and distress I did this, the Lord is my best witness.'

In one of his letters he put it even more strongly: 'I would rather submit to death a hundred times rather than to that cross, on which one had to perish daily a thousand times over.' He wrote to Farel, who had advised him to return to Geneva, 'Had I the choice at my disposal, nothing would be less agreeable to me than to follow your advice.' But Calvin admitted that 'the more I baulked at returning, the more suspicious I became of myself.'

After struggling for months with the call from Geneva, Calvin determined to accept it. Left to himself he would not return to Geneva, he wrote to Farel, then added, 'but when I remember that I am not my own, I offer up my heart, presented as a sacrifice to the Lord', thus following in his own life the words he had written in the new edition of his *Institutes*. 'We are not our own: let not our reason nor our will, therefore, sway our plans and deeds. We are not our own: let us therefore not set it as our goal to seek what is expedient for us according to the flesh. We are not our own: in so far as we can, let us therefore forget ourselves and all that is ours. Conversely, we are God's: let us therefore live for him and die for him. We are God's: let his wisdom and will therefore rule all our actions. We are God's: let all the parts of our life accordingly strive toward him as our only lawful goal.'

Calvin designed his own seal, a flaming heart on an outstretched hand with the words, 'My heart, I give to you, O Lord, promptly and sincerely.' His testimony and his earnest desire were summed up by that seal and motto.[8]

John Calvin left Strasbourg in tears and entered Geneva on September 13, 1541. The Register of the Company of Pastors noted that John Calvin, 'minister of the gospel', had arrived and 'offered himself to be always the servant of Geneva'. His first Sunday back in the church in Geneva, Calvin opened the Bible at the same page at which he had left off three and a half years earlier, read the next passage as his text, and preached from it. Calvin explained: 'When I went before the people to preach everyone was prey to great curiosity. But passing over in complete silence the events which everyone assuredly expected me to mention, I stated in a few words the principles of my ministry, then with brevity and discretion recalled the faith and integrity that animated me. After this introduction I chose the text to comment on in the same place where I had stopped before. I wanted to show by this that rather than having laid down the duty of teaching, I had been interrupted in it for a time'.

'God still wishes in these days to build his spiritual temple amidst the anxieties of the times.'

Calvin gave himself unstintingly to leading the church in Geneva toward a renewed faith and strengthened devotion to God—in catechisms and theological writings, sermons, biblical commentaries, liturgies, psalms and prayers, pastoral instructions, and letters of counsel and consolation. Calvin wrote that a minister 'will never steadfastly persevere in this office unless the love of Christ so reigns in his heart that forgetting himself and devoting himself entirely to him, he surmounts every obstacle'. In his *Commentary on Daniel*, Calvin described the challenges he faced as a minister of the church: 'Although God's loving kindness to us was wonderful when the pure gospel emerged out of that dreadful darkness in which it had been buried for so many ages, our affairs are still troubled. The impious still ceaselessly and furiously oppose the unhappy church, both by the sword and the virulence of their tongues. Internal enemies use covert arts in their schemes to subvert our edifice; wicked men destroy all order and interpose many obstacles to impede our progress. But God still wishes in these days to build his spiritual temple amidst the anxieties of the times. The faithful must still hold the trowel in one hand and the sword in the other, because the building of the church must still be combined with many struggles.'

With 'the trowel in one hand and the sword in the other', Calvin worked to build God's church in Geneva and beyond. He saw himself, not as a reformer or theologian, but as a preacher and pastor. A glance at these two major tasks of Calvin's gives us greater insight into his testimony.

'Let him who speaks, speak only the words of God.'

T. H. L. Parker aptly describes John Calvin's preaching as 'the quiet, persistent call to frame our lives according to the teaching of Holy Scripture ... There is no threshing himself into a fever of impatience or frustration, no holier-than-thou rebuking of the people, no begging them in terms of hyperbole to give some physical sign that the message has been accepted. It is simply one man, conscious of his sins, aware how little progress he makes and how hard it is to be a doer of the word, sympathetically passing on to his people (whom he knows to have the same sort of problems as himself) what God has said to them and to him.'[9]

When he preached, Calvin told his congregation, 'I am not here for myself alone. It is true that we should all profit in common, for when I mount to the pulpit it is not to teach others only. I do not withdraw myself apart, since I should be a student, and the word that proceeds from my mouth should serve me as well as you, or it is the worse for me.' In a sermon on 2 Timothy 3:16-17, Calvin said that the goal of preaching is not to make us 'eloquent and subtle and I know not what. It is to reform our life, so that it is known that we desire to serve God, to give ourselves entirely to him and to conform ourselves to his good will.'

In the *Institutes*, Calvin used the words of 1 Peter 4:11 to describe the task and the power of the preacher: 'Peter, who was well instructed by the Master as to how much he should do, reserves nothing else for himself or others except to impart the doctrine as it has been handed down by God. "Let him who speaks," he says, "speak only the words of God." Here, then, is the sovereign power with which the pastors of the church, by whatever name they be called, ought to be endowed. That is that they may dare boldly to do all things by God's word; may compel all worldly power, glory, wisdom, and exaltation to yield to and obey his majesty; supported by his power; may command all from the highest even to the last; may build up Christ's household and cast down Satan's; may feed the sheep and drive away the wolves; may instruct and exhort the teachable; may accuse, rebuke, and subdue the rebellious and stubborn; may bind and loose; finally, if need be, may launch thunderbolts and lightnings; but do all things in God's word.'

'I do not see that any excuse will avail us if we are found wanting in the discharge of our duty where we are most needed.'

Calvin was not only a preacher, he was a pastor. Given his self-confessed diffident and retiring personality, it must have been difficult for Calvin to become closely involved in the lives of people. He did it nonetheless. Martin Bucer wrote to him: 'I must greatly praise you for visiting the brethren, for you know with what pain I have observed that the duty of piety and love, on the part of the clergy—to visit, warn, and comfort the people—is greatly neglected.'

Through continuing conflict with a host of enemies, acute and enduring physical suffering, the premature birth and death of his son, and the death of his wife, Calvin learned how to suffer with those who suffered. 'When I first received the intelligence of the death of your son Louis,' Calvin wrote to a friend, 'I was so utterly overpowered that for many days I was fit for nothing but to grieve.' Calvin wrote to someone in sorrow, 'Speaking of love, St Paul never forgets that it is fitting for us to weep with those who weep; that is, if we are Christian, we must have such compassion and sympathy for our neighbours that we would freely bear part of their grief in order to ease them somewhat.' After the death of a Frenchwoman in Geneva, Calvin wrote a long letter to a friend of hers reporting the sad news and asking her to inform the woman's father. 'Our consolation is that he has gathered her unto himself,' he wrote, 'for he has guided her even to the last sigh, as if visibly he had held out a hand to her.'

In her research in the archives in Geneva, Jeannine Olson discovered a much more friendly and accessible Calvin than the one often pictured. He comes across, she asserts, 'as humane, cordial, concerned, even warm'.[10] Mary Beaty and Benjamin W. Farley, translators and editors of Calvin's *Ecclesiastical Advice*, also found a friendly, approachable, pastoral Calvin, at least as a rule, even in his handling of the complex and controversial matters of church polity and discipline. They write that 'the advice contained in these pieces portrays the familiar reformer whom Calvinists have come to know and expect, occasionally surprising his readers with the depth of his compassion and wit, patience and rigour'.[11] 'Countless friends and strangers made his house their hostel,' commented John T. McNeill. One of these wrote to him afterwards: 'Your hospitality in the name of Christ is not unknown to anybody in Europe.'[12]

One of Calvin's colleagues in Geneva wrote: 'No words of mine can declare the fidelity and prudence with which he gave counsel, the kindness with which he received all who came to him, the clearness and promptitude with which he replied to those who asked his opinion on the most important questions, and the ability with which he disentangled the difficulties and problems which were laid before him. Nor can I express the gentleness with which he could comfort the afflicted and raise the fallen and the distressed.'[13]

When the plague came to Geneva in 1542, the council forbade him to visit its victims, but Calvin insisted that he too be available for this work. He explained to Viret that 'so long as we are in this ministry, I do not see that any excuse will avail us if, through fear of infection, we are found wanting in the discharge of our duty where we are most needed'.

'God calls me in his name to see to it that lies are suppressed.'

Preaching the word of God and serving the people of God (and others) are the great tasks of gospel ministers. Also,

Calvin believed that the truth of the Bible must be defended at all costs. The minister has the trowel in one hand to build the church, and the sword in the other to protect it from its enemies.

Preaching on the ninth commandment, John Calvin said: 'When I see truth oppressed, to the best of my ability, I must not tolerate it. Why? Because God calls me in his name to see to it that lies are suppressed. And above all, this applies with respect to the doctrine of salvation. Let us learn that when we live with men in such simplicity that people cannot reproach us for wanting to denigrate anyone, either by calumny, or lies, or slander, we ought also to maintain this same zeal with respect to God, that his truth abide in its fullness and that it may be maintained in order for his reign to be active in our midst.'

In his reply to Sadoleto, Calvin explained why he wrote what he did: 'If you had attacked me in my private character, I could easily have forgiven the attack in consideration of your learning, and in honour of letters. But when I see that my ministry, which I feel assured is supported and sanctioned by a call from God, is wounded through my side, it would be perfidy, not patience, were I here to be silent and connive. I am compelled, whether I will or not, to withstand you openly. For then only do pastors edify the Church, when, besides leading docile souls to Christ placidly, as with the hand, they are also armed to repel the machinations of those who strive to impede the work of God.'

Calvin was committed to defending the faith against numerous opponents, because he believed that those who are 'poisoners of souls' do 'a thing much more heinous and detestable than if they had murdered their bodies'. Just as clearly, he did not enjoy it. 'There is something in Luther and Knox that made them capable of delight in conflict,' writes John T. McNeill, but 'Calvin winced with sensitivity and apprehension, even while to opponents he appeared hard as steel.'[14]

My letters are 'the living image of my soul'.

Calvin's ministry of counsel, correction, and encouragement reached beyond Geneva through his extensive correspondence (eleven volumes of his collected writings) with a wide range of people—royalty, men and women imprisoned for their faith, people troubled by personal and theological issues, and church leaders of many countries. Calvin's correspondence reveals his mind and heart about many things, thereby giving us something more of his testimony. Calvin saw his letters as 'the living image of my soul', so that, according to Selderhuis, 'the real Calvin is to be found in his correspondence'.[15] J. I. Packer has written, 'As his pastoral letters show, Calvin was a superb physician of the soul, unerring in diagnosis and supremely skillful in applying the remedies of the gospel.'[16] Ronald Wallace comments that for Calvin, 'each soul is new, each situation is new, and God's way must always be found out afresh'.[17]

W. de Greef writes that Calvin's letters 'give us the opportunity to get to know him personally in his interaction with others ... He corresponded especially often with his colleagues Guillaume Farel in Neuchâtel, Pierre Viret in Lausanne, and Heinrich Bullinger in Zurich. He also wrote many pastoral letters to people in one sort of crisis or another to provide them with spiritual support in their particular circumstances. He often urged those in high positions who were trying to serve the Lord to stay on the course that they had adopted.'[18]

Calvin dedicated his *Commentary on Titus* to Farel and Viret. He compared their work in Neuchâtel and Lausanne to Paul's on Crete, and wrote, 'I do not think there have ever been such friends who have ever lived in such close friendship as we have in our ministry.'

In a letter to Viret on May 19, 1540, Calvin teased his friend for recommending to him that he return to Geneva for the sake of his health! 'Why could you not have said at the cross? For it would have been far preferable to perish once for all than to be tormented again in that place of torture!' Seriously, Calvin wrote that he could scarcely persuade himself that he was 'worth so much trouble', but was glad for 'the kindness of good men' toward him.

Many of Calvin's letters were to William Farel, whom he called his 'most sound-hearted brother'. He promised Farel that he would always be candid with him; he would 'not appear to be looking in one direction and rowing in another'. When Farel was nearly seventy he married a girl not yet sixteen and incurred Calvin's severe rebuke. Calvin, however, pleaded with the ministers of Neuchâtel, entreating them 'to remember how he has employed himself, during the space of thirty-six years and more, in serving God and edifying his church, how profitable his labours have been, and with what zeal he laboured'. The friendship of Calvin and Farel survived. Calvin wrote to Farel, drawing from the death of an esteemed pastor a call for them to carry on in the work God had given them. 'We, the survivors whom the Lord has left behind for a while, let us persevere in the same path wherein our deceased brother walked until we have finished our course.'

Calvin and Melanchthon became close friends. In their correspondence Calvin gently but firmly encouraged the Lutheran to manifest greater decision and firmness but strongly supported him in his effort 'to recall the minds of men from strife and contention'. Calvin acknowledged that 'where there exists so much division and separation as we now see, it is indeed no easy matter to still the troubled waters and bring about composure'. He closed this letter to his friend with words of encouragement for them both: 'Howbeit let us wait patiently for a peaceable conclusion, such as it shall please the Lord to vouchsafe. In the meanwhile, let us run the race set before us with deliberate courage. I return you very many thanks for your reply, and at the same time, for the extraordinary kindness which Claude [one of Calvin's colleagues in Geneva] assures me had been shown to him by you. I can form a conjecture what you would have been to myself, from your having given so kind and courteous a reception to my friend.' In another letter to Melanchthon, Calvin writes that he looked forward eagerly to their 'feasting together in heaven'.

Calvin loved and respected his fellow Protestants, above all Martin Luther, but also some that Luther bitterly denounced. After Luther's violent pamphlet against the Swiss Reformers in 1544, Calvin wrote to Melanchthon, 'I reverence him but I am ashamed of him.' In his only letter to Luther, Calvin wrote that he wished for a few hours of conversation with him. 'But seeing that it is not granted to us on earth, I hope that shortly it will come to pass in the kingdom of God. Adieu, most renowned sir, most distinguished minister of Christ, and my ever-honoured father. The Lord himself rule and direct you by his own Spirit, that you may persevere even unto the end for the common benefit and good of his own church.'[19]

Calvin often expressed his concern that he and other Reformers observe moderation in many things, while attempting to be faithful to the Bible's directions in all things. He wrote to the Duke of Somerset, regent of England under the minority of Edward VI: 'I willingly acknowledge that we must observe moderation, and that overdoing is neither discreet or useful; indeed, that forms of worship need to be accommodated to the condition and tastes of the people.'

But he warns that 'there are some who, under the pretence of moderation, are in favour of sparing many abuses.'

Calvin deplored the controversy and division over the liturgy in the church of English refugees at Frankfurt: 'This indeed grievously afflicts me and is highly absurd, that discord is springing up among brethren who are for the same faith exiles and fugitives from their country. Though in indifferent matters, such as external rites, I show myself indulgent and pliable, at the same time I do not deem it expedient always to comply with the foolish captiousness of those who will not give up a single point of their usual routine.'

Calvin wrote to John Knox that he rejoiced in the news that the gospel had made 'such rapid and happy progress' in Scotland but added a caution: 'With regard to ceremonies of worship, I trust, even should you displease many, that you will moderate your rigour. You are well aware that certain things should be tolerated even if you do not quite approve of them.'

Calvin wrote to Thomas Cranmer that one of the chief evils of the time was the division of the churches: 'The very heaviest blame attaches to the leaders themselves who, either engrossed in their own sinful pursuits, are indifferent to the safety and entire piety of the Church, or who, individually satisfied with their own private peace, have no regard for others. Thus it is that the members of the Church being severed, the body lies bleeding. So much does this concern me that could I be of any service, I would not grudge to cross even ten seas, if need were, on account of it.'

Not only did Calvin write to leaders of church and state, he responded to requests for help and advice from ordinary people. He took the time to encourage a young student at the University of Padua who had written to him: 'I could not give a fitter expression of my love towards you, than by exhorting and encouraging you first of all to give devoted submission to the will of the Lord, and in the next place, you must fortify yourself by his sacred doctrines. I wish very much you could find it convenient at some time to pay us a visit; for, I flatter myself, you would never regret the journey. Whatever you do, see that you follow the Lord, and at no time turn aside from the chief end.'

'I write, worn out with sadness, and not without tears.'

Calvin wrote to a woman who was suffering: 'Our illnesses are surely not only to humble us by showing us our weakness, but they should also encourage us to examine ourselves so as to acknowledge our weakness and take refuge in God's mercy. They should also serve as remedies that free us from the desires of this world and burn away all that is unnecessary. Further, they are messages from death that ought to teach us to lift one foot, ready to leave when God so desires.'

In a letter to Farel Calvin revealed the depths of his own grief at the death of Augustin Courault, a zealous preacher of the Reformation at Paris and Geneva. Calvin wrote: 'The death of Courault has so overwhelmed me, that I can set no bounds to my grief. None of my daily occupations can so avail to engage my mind as that they do not seem to turn upon that one thought. Distress and wretchedness during the day seems only to prepare a lodging for the more painful and excruciating thoughts of the night.'

As he so often did, Calvin followed matters of great sorrow with words of exhortation and encouragement. He ended this letter to Farel: 'We, the survivors whom the Lord has left behind for a while, let us persevere in the same path wherein our deceased brother walked until we have finished our course. Whatsoever difficulties may be thrown across our path, they will not prevent our arriving at that rest into which he has been already admitted. Unless this sure hope held us firm and steadfast, what ground of despair encompasses us round about! But since the truth of the Lord remains firm and unshaken, let us stand resolutely upon the watch-tower even to the end, until the kingdom of Christ, which is now hidden and obscured, may shine forth.'

Jean-Daniel Benoit writes that 'Calvin was a pastor and counsellor for martyrs! This is one light in which he is too little known. However, perhaps this facet of his career reveals the genuine depth of his life and is the clearest illustration of his piety.'[20]

In writing to Farel about the suffering of Waldensians, Calvin closed with the words: 'I write, worn out with sadness, and not without tears, which so burst forth that every now and then they interrupt my words.'

Calvin wrote to the persecuted Christians in France: 'For in prosperity we do not experience the worth of his assistance and the power of his Spirit, as when we are oppressed by men. That seems strange to us; but he who sees more clearly than we, knows far better what is advantageous for us. Now when he permits his children to be afflicted, there is no doubt but that it is for their good. Thus we are forced to conclude that whatever he orders is the best thing we could desire.'

Calvin wrote four lengthy letters to five young Frenchmen who went from Lausanne, where they had studied, to France as missionaries. They were arrested, imprisoned, and finally condemned to the stake on March 1, 1553. In these letters we see Calvin's concern, compassion, and care for suffering people, along with his unbroken trust in God who does all things right.

'I beseech our good Lord that he would be pleased to make you feel in every way the worth of his protection of his own, to fill you with his Holy Spirit, who gives you prudence and virtue, and brings you peace, joy, and contentment; and may the name of our Lord Jesus be glorified by you to the edification of his Church!'

'It cannot be but that you feel some twinges of frailty; yet, be confident that he whose service you are upon will so rule in your hearts by his Holy Spirit, that his grace shall overcome all temptations. We who are here shall do our duty in praying that he would glorify himself more and more by your constancy, and that he may, by the consolation of his Spirit, sweeten and endear all that is bitter to the flesh, and so absorb your spirits in himself, that in contemplating that heavenly crown, you may be ready without regret to leave all that belongs to this world.

'Since it pleases God to employ you to the death in maintaining his quarrel, he will strengthen your hands in the fight, and will not suffer a single drop of your blood to be spent in vain. And though the fruit may not all at once appear, yet in time it shall spring up more abundantly than we can express.'

'I am a stranger in this city.'

Calvin's pastoral life in Geneva was not an easy one. He said to friends as he and William Farel were being harried out of town in 1538: 'Certainly, had I been the servant of men I had obtained a poor reward, but it is well that I have served him, who never fails to perform to his servants whatever he has promised.' Calvin returned to Geneva, but after living there almost twenty years, he wrote, 'I am a stranger in this city.' He was threatened, dismayed, and almost overcome by the opposition and even hatred that his ministry provoked.

Calvin wrote to Farel in May 1544, 'I begin to learn again what it means to live in Geneva! I am in the midst of the thorns.' He wrote in a preface to the *Institutes* of 1559, 'I think that there is no one who is assailed, bitten, and wounded by more false accusations than I.' He told his friends: 'If I had thought only of my own life and my private interests I would have immediately gone elsewhere. But when I think of the importance of this corner of the earth for the propagation of the kingdom of Christ, it is with reason that I occupy myself with defending it.'[21]

'A pilot steers the ship in which we sail.'

When Calvin's troubles began to mount, so did his conviction that God had placed him in Geneva. In a time of crisis in 1553 Calvin preached what he thought might be his last sermon in the city. He said: 'As for me, while God keeps me here, since he has given me constancy and I have taken it from him, I will use it, whatever happens, and will govern myself only by the rules of my master, which are clear and obvious to me. Since we should now receive the Holy Communion of our Lord Jesus Christ, if anyone wants to intrude at this holy table to whom it has been forbidden by the consistory of the church, it is certain that I will show myself, at the risk of my life, what I should be. As for me I would rather have been killed than have offered the holy things of God with this hand to those declared guilty as scorners.'

Theodore Beza described what happened: 'The sermon had been preached, the prayers had been offered, and Calvin descended from the pulpit to take his place beside the elements at the communion table. The bread and wine were duly consecrated by him, and he was now ready to distribute them to the communicants. Then on a sudden a rush was begun by the troublers in Israel in the direction of the communion table. Calvin flung his arms around the sacramental vessels as if to protect them from sacrilege, while his voice rang through the building: "These hands you may crush, these arms you may cut off, my life you may take, my blood is yours, you may shed it; but you shall never force me to give holy things to be profaned, and dishonour the table of my God.'"

The immediate crisis passed, but Calvin preached that afternoon on Paul's farewell address to the elders of Ephesus. His text was Acts 20:32, 'Now I commit you to God and to the word of his grace.' Calvin told the people: 'You know after what manner I have been with you at all seasons, serving the Lord with all humility Neither count I my life dear unto myself, so that I might finish my course and the ministry, which I have received of the Lord Jesus.'

During the difficult and threatening days of 1553, Calvin encouraged himself and Farel with confidence in God's presence: 'Although we may be severely buffeted hither and thither by many tempests, yet, seeing that a pilot steers the ship in which we sail, who will never allow us to perish even in the midst of shipwrecks, there is no reason why our minds should be overwhelmed with fear and overcome with weariness.'

'I take pains to live in such a way that my character and conduct do not conflict with what I teach.'

Writing on 1 Corinthians 9:27 Calvin paraphrased the verse as follows: 'My life ought to provide some sort of example to others. Therefore I take pains to live in such a way that my character and conduct do not conflict with what I teach.' Commenting on 1 Peter 5:1-4, Calvin explained that pastors must not only be orthodox in doctrine but also must strive to make themselves 'examples to the flock', that is, 'they are to excel for the purpose of being eminent in holiness'. Calvin deplored the fact that pastors, who should 'surpass all others in the purity of their lives', sometimes failed to do so and thus compromised their message so that it possessed 'no more truth and seriousness than if a player were acting out a tale on the stage'. Some pastors, Calvin said, 'boldly exalt the dignity of the ministry, but it does not enter their heads that their esteem for the ministry is not accepted because they defile it by their own disgraceful conduct. Someone once truly said, "In order to be loved, be loving." In the same way those who wish to be appreciated need to gain respect by the seriousness and sanctity of their behaviour.'

Calvin noted three vices that especially tempt pastors—sloth, desire for gain, and lust for power—and urged, as Peter does, hard work, a generous spirit, and a humble heart.

Sloth was not one of Calvin's vices. In fact, he could probably be faulted for working too much. Calvin himself

warned that men 'wear themselves out and torment themselves in vain, when they are more busy than their calling
permits or compels'. He may have been thinking of himself
when he remarked in a sermon that 'a great many people
are their own executioners through working constantly and
without measure'. When he was dying Calvin refused to
cease his laborious work on his Ezekiel commentary. Urged
by friends to rest, he replied, 'Would you have the Lord find
me idle?' He finally stopped dictating about eight hours
before he died, when his voice gave out. Calvin certainly
lived what he wrote while commenting on Luke 17:7: 'Let
each of us remember that he has been created by God for
the purpose of labouring, and of being vigorously employed
in his work, and that not only for a limited time, but till
death itself, and what is more, that he should not only live,
but die, to God.'

A desire for gain did not tempt Calvin. He informed
Sadoleto that he and his fellow reformers 'counselled that as
much should be distributed to ministers as might suffice for
a frugal life befitting their order without luxurious super-
abundance', and that beyond that the money of the church
be used to help the poor.

When Calvin was accused of using his position in
Geneva to enrich himself, he replied: 'All of Geneva and the
surrounding areas know that I do not own even a square
inch of property. We use furniture that belongs to someone
else. Neither the table from which we eat, nor the bed in

which we sleep, is ours.' 'Everyone knows,' Calvin continued, 'I turned down an offer of a raise, and did so with such persistence that I swore under oath that I would not preach a single sermon more if they did not stop offering it.'

When Calvin left Strasbourg to return to Geneva in 1541, Martin Bucer and the Strasbourg magistrates urged him to keep his Strasbourg citizenship and his salary. He declined the salary but happily remained a citizen of Strasbourg. It was not until Christmas Day 1559 that Calvin became a citizen of Geneva. When Calvin died, Pope Pius IV is said to have commented that Calvin's strength lay in the fact that he could never be corrupted by money.[22]

Although he is falsely maligned as the dictator of Geneva, Calvin never sought personal power. John T. McNeill sets the record straight. 'Calvin went unarmed and unguarded, lived modestly and without display, sought advice from many, claimed no authority save as a commissioned minister of the word, assumed no title of distinction or political office.'[23]

'I am perfectly aware that my temper is naturally inclined to be violent.'

There was one sin, however, that Calvin struggled with, and he knew it. A few weeks after his calm and respectful letter to Sadoleto, someone charged Calvin with anti-trinitarian heresy. Calvin let himself go in a fit of anger. He confessed in a letter to Farel: 'I have sinned grievously in not having been able to keep within bounds. I poured out bitterness on all sides. When I returned home, I was suddenly completely overwhelmed. I could find no comfort, and only sighed and cried.'

Later Calvin rebuked a friend for his excessive anger in conflict with a colleague but reminded him that 'these counsels are given you by a man, who, though he is conscious of possessing a more vehement temper than he could wish', was learning to bear more patiently similar aggravations. When someone complained about Calvin's anger, he replied, 'I take it kindly of you to exhort me to moderation. I am perfectly aware that my temper is naturally inclined to be violent.'

Calvin struggled with this problem all his life, and in his farewell words to the leaders, pastors, and people of Geneva, he asked forgiveness for his anger and violent expressions. It is easy to find many examples of Calvin's strong language against his opponents and even his friends, but there are also examples of his kindness and generosity.

When Louis du Tillet, a friend since their days together in Paris, returned to the Roman Catholic Church, Calvin was deeply hurt, but he ended his letter warmly: 'I entreat you to have special remembrance of us in your prayers, to which although the knowledge you have of our weakness ought sufficiently to stir you up; nevertheless, the difficulties which press upon us ought yet more to arouse you, as they are now greater than ever. After humbly commending myself to your kind remembrance, I pray the Lord to keep you in his holy protection.'[24]

Calvin wrote a letter to Laelius Socinus in which he politely declined to engage in further correspondence about what he called 'airy speculations'. He explained: 'Certainly no one can be more averse to paradox than I am, and in subtleties I find no delight at all. Yet nothing shall ever hinder me from openly avowing what I have learned from the word of God; for nothing but what is useful is taught in the school of this master. It is my only guide, and to acquiesce in its plain doctrines shall be my constant rule of wisdom. Would that you also, my dear Laelius, would learn to regulate your powers with the same moderation! You have no reason to expect a reply from me so long as you bring forward those monstrous questions.'

Calvin closed his letter to Socinus, who eventually became one of the leaders of a rationalist movement that was the forerunner of modern Unitarianism, with kind words: 'Adieu, brother very highly esteemed by me; and if this rebuke is harsher than it ought to be, ascribe it to my love to you.'

In his reply to Sadoleto, Calvin included a beautiful prayer for the cardinal and his Church: 'The Lord grant, Sadoleto, that you and all your party may at length perceive that the only true bond of ecclesiastical unity would exist if Christ the Lord, who has reconciled us to God the Father, were to gather us out of our present dispersion into the fellowship of his body, that so, through his one word and Spirit, we might join together with one heart and one soul.'

'It is good that we are anchored in heaven.'

Looking back at his life, John Calvin spoke words of testimony: 'From my very birth, God has cared for me. I have gone through a million dangers, and he has delivered me. And would I then not repay my Father for his protection? I further have been oppressed on every side, but God always took heed of me. And how often have I not become Satan's prey, and yet God did not a single time will that I should perish?'

Calvin's illness forced him, much to his sorrow, to reduce his work. In February 1564, he wrote to the physicians of Montpellier, thanking them for their interest in his serious condition. 'I have no other means of testifying my gratitude to you,' Calvin wrote, 'besides that of recommending you to draw in your turn from my writings what may afford you a spiritual medicine.' He closed his letters to the doctors with a benediction: 'Farewell, most accomplished sirs, whom I sincerely honour. May the Lord always direct you by his Spirit, sustain you by his power, and enrich you more and more with his gifts.'

On one occasion Calvin wrote rather darkly: 'If you look carefully you will see that things are such that someone who gets up in the morning cannot take a step, cannot eat a meal and cannot move a hand without continually becoming older. Life becomes shorter. For that reason we must simply acknowledge that our life disappears in the blink of an eye and flows away. We are always heading toward death, it comes near to us, and we must in the end go to it.'

More characteristic of Calvin are some words he wrote in 1552: 'It is good that we are anchored in heaven, for otherwise we would never be able to sail safely through these storms.'

'I trust that God out of his infinite goodness will permit me to persevere with unwavering patience in the path of his holy calling.'

In a short preface for the last edition of the *Institutes*, Calvin expressed his gratitude for how the earlier editions had been received and felt that he 'was much more favoured' than he deserved. He wrote: 'I can furnish a very clear testimony of my great zeal and effort to carry out this task for God's church. Last winter when I thought the quartan fever was summoning me to my death, the more the disease pressed upon me the less I spared myself, until I could leave a book behind me that might, in some measure, repay the generous invitation of godly men. I trust that God out of his infinite goodness will permit me to persevere with unwavering patience in the path of his holy calling. In this edition I set forth new proof of this fact for godly readers.'

John Calvin had only a few more years to walk in the path of God's 'holy calling'. In his last months we find more of his testimony, as he summed up his life, said goodbye to friends and colleagues, and looked forward to heaven. Calvin preached for the last time on February 6, 1564. He gave his last lecture a few days later, leaving his series on Ezekiel unfinished. He ended his commentary at Ezekiel 20:44 and with a prayer: 'Almighty God, we have already entered in hope upon the threshold of our eternal inheritance, and know that there is a mansion for us in heaven since Christ, our head and the first fruits of our salvation, has been received there. Grant that we may proceed more and more in the way of your holy calling until at length we reach the goal and so enjoy the eternal glory of which you have given us a taste in this world, by the same Christ our Lord. Amen.'

'I, John Calvin, minister of the word of God in the Church of Geneva, render thanks to God.'

On April 25, Calvin dictated his last will and testament, including in it his last testimony. 'In the name of God, I, John Calvin, minister of the word of God in the Church of Geneva, render thanks to God, not only because he has had compassion on me, his poor creature, to draw me out of the abyss of idolatry in which I was plunged, in order to bring me to the light of his gospel and make me a partaker of the doctrine of salvation, of which I was altogether unworthy, and continuing his mercy he has supported me amid so many sins and shortcomings, which were such that I well deserved to be rejected by him a hundred thousand times—but what is more, he has so far extended his mercy towards me as to make use of me and of my labour, to convey and announce the truth of his gospel; protesting [to make a solemn declaration or affirmation] that it is my wish to live and die in this faith which he has bestowed on me, having no other hope nor refuge except in his gratuitous adoption, upon which all my salvation is founded; embracing the grace which he has given me in our Lord Jesus Christ, and accepting the merits of his death and passion, in order that by this means all my sins may be buried; and praying him so to wash and cleanse me by the blood of this great Redeemer, which has been shed for us poor sinners, that I may appear before his face, bearing as it were his image.

'I protest also that I have endeavoured, according to the measure of grace he has given me, to teach his word in purity, both in my sermons and writings, and to expound faithfully the Holy Scriptures; and moreover, that in all the disputes I have had with the enemies of the truth, I have never made use of subtle craft nor sophistry, but have gone to work straightforwardly in maintaining his quarrel. But alas! the desire which I have had, and the zeal, if so it must be called, has been so cold and so sluggish that I feel myself a debtor in everything and everywhere, and that were it not for his infinite goodness, all the affection I have had would be but as smoke, nay, that even the favours which he has accorded me would but render me so much the more guilty;

so that my only recourse is this, that being the Father of mercies he will show himself the Father of so miserable a sinner.'

'I have had many infirmities which you have been obliged to bear with.'

On April 27, John Calvin bade farewell to the seigneurs of Geneva who had gathered at his house. He thanked them, saying that 'they had been pleased to do him more honour than was due to him, and to bear with him in many circumstances in which he stood in great need of their indulgence'. He told them that he had 'desired the good of this city', but added that he was 'far from having accomplished all his duty in respect to it'. He confessed 'his natural disposition, too vehement by far, and with which he was offended, and with his other vices'. He closed his farewell with words of exhortation and a prayer for God 'to conduct and govern us, continually increasing his grace in us, and causing it to turn to our own salvation and that of all this poor people'.

The next day, Calvin bid farewell to the ministers of Geneva. He began with prayer, 'in order that God may give me grace to say everything without ambition, always having a respect to his glory, and also that every one may retain and profit by what shall be said'. Calvin talked about his illness, his early experiences in Geneva and Strasbourg, and Geneva again. He encouraged his fellow pastors to 'take courage and fortify yourselves, for God will make use of this church and will maintain it, and assures you that he will protect it'.

He told the ministers: 'I have had many infirmities which you have been obliged to bear with but certainly I can say this, that I have willed what is good, that my vices have always displeased me, and that the root of the fear of God has been in my heart. I have written nothing out of hatred to anyone, but I have always faithfully propounded what I esteemed to be for the glory of God.'

'A wall between us will not prevent me from being joined in spirit with you.'

On May 2, John Calvin sent a last letter to William Farel. 'Farewell, my most excellent and upright brother; and since it is the will of God that you should survive me in the world, live mindful of our intimacy, which, as it was useful to the church of God, so the fruits of it await us in heaven. I am unwilling that you should fatigue yourself for my sake. I draw my breath with difficulty, and every moment I am in expectation of breathing my last. It is enough that I live and die for Christ, who is to all his followers a gain in life and death. Again I bid you and your brethren Farewell.'

On May 4, Theodore Beza wrote that 'our father and the faithful servant of God' is near death. 'As he had afforded us a rare example of an upright life, so now he furnishes us with one of a courageous and truly Christian death.'[25]

On May 19 Calvin shared a last meal with his fellow ministers. Beza wrote: 'He himself gave the prayer as he best could and forced himself to entertain us, although he could eat very little. Before the end of the supper he took leave and had himself carried back to his room, which was nearby, saying these words with the happiest expression he could: "A wall between us will not prevent me from being joined in spirit with you."'

'Gone to God.'

In the minutes of the Consistory of Geneva there is a simple cross beside Calvin's name and the words: 'Gone to God, May 27th of the present year, between 8 and 9 o'clock, p.m.' In Geneva citizens and strangers mourned for him, while the Little Council in special session declared: 'God marked him with a character of singular majesty.' The body of John Calvin was buried in an unmarked grave in a quiet cemetery in Geneva. That is what he wanted.

Endnotes

1 Heiko A. Oberman, *Luther: Man Between God and the Devil* (New York: Doubleday, 1992), 312.

2 John Calvin, *Commentary on the Book of Psalms*, trans. James Anderson (Grand Rapids: Wm. B. Eerdmans Publishing Company, 1949). *Letters of John Calvin*, ed. Jules Bonnet (Philadelphia: Presbyterian Board of Publication, 1858; repr. Edinburgh: Banner of

Truth Trust, 2009, in a seven-volume set, *John Calvin, Tracts and Letters*). A judicious selection of Calvin's letters from the Bonnet edition was published by The Banner of Truth Trust. Calvin's Reply to Sadoleto can be found in a number of places, including *A Reformation Debate: Sadoleto's Letter to the Genevans and Calvin's Reply*, ed. John C. Olin (New York: Harper & Row, 1966). Calvin's Reply to Sadoleto and the preface to his Psalms commentary are harmonized by Ford Lewis Battles in Appendix 1 ('The Chief Lineaments of Calvin's Religious Experience') in *Interpreting John Calvin* (Grand Rapids: Baker Books, 1996). Citations and references to the original sources (Latin and French) have also been gleaned from a number of books about Calvin.

[3] Elsie Anne McKee, ed., *John Calvin: Writings on Pastoral Piety* (New York: Paulist Press, 2001), 18.

[4] Bernard Cottret, *Calvin: A Biography* (Grand Rapids: Wm B. Eerdmans, 2000), 70.

[5] Calvin came to appreciate and respect both Oecolampadius and Zwingli. He paid deep-felt homage to the memory of these 'excellent' men in a letter to Bullinger on March 4, 1538.

[6] John T. McNeill, *The History and Character of Calvinism* (London: Oxford University Press, 1954), 117-18.

[7] Cottret, *Calvin*, 152. Even Luther was impressed. He wrote to Bucer in October, 1539 that he had read Calvin's reply 'with unusual pleasure'.

[8] John A. Mackay, in *Christianity on the Frontier* (New York: Macmillan, 1950), and writes: 'The most relevant symbol for Reformed thought and action today is John Calvin's crest of the flaming heart in the outstretched hand' (92).

[9] T. H. L. Parker, *Calvin's Preaching* (Louisville: Westminster/John Knox Press, 1992), 118–19.

[10] Jeannine Olson, 'Calvin as Person', *Concordia Journal* (October 1991), 393.

[11] *Calvin's Ecclesiastical Advice*, trans. Mary Beaty and Benjamin W. Farley (Louisville: Westminster/John Knox Press, 1991), 13.

[12] John T. McNeill, *Calvinism* (London: Oxford University Press, 1954), 231.

[13] Quoted by Ronald S. Wallace, *Calvin, Geneva and the Reformation: A Story of Calvin as Social Reformer, Churchman, Pastor and Theologian* (Grand Rapids: Baker, 1988), 180-1.

[14] McNeill, *Calvinism*, 171.

[15] Herman J. Selderhuis, *John Calvin: A Pilgrim's Life* (Downers Grove, IL: IVP Academic, 2009), 165.

[16] J. I. Packer, 'Calvin: A Servant of the Word', in *Able Ministers of the New Testament: Papers Read at the Puritan and Reformed Studies Conference, December 1964*. In a long article titled 'Calvin's Ministry of Encouragement', Ian M. Tait has collected many examples of Calvin's pastoral counsel from his letters: 'Calvin's Ministry of Encouragement' (*Presbyterion: Covenant Seminary Review* 11 [1985]: 43-99).

[17] Wallace, *Calvin, Geneva and the Reformation*, 179.

[18] W. de Greef, *The Writings of John Calvin: An Introductory Guide* (Grand Rapids: Baker Books, 1993), 210.

[19] *Letters of John Calvin*, 73.

[20] Jean-Daniel Benoit, *Calvin, Directeur d'âmes* (Strasbourg: Oberlin, 1947), 61.

[21] 'Geneva, a city of some 10,000 people with little claim to distinction (it had no university, no major printing house and no leading industries or financial institutions) but strategically placed for trade and communications, became through the Reformation a centre of international importance in religion, higher education and publishing. This transformation is a measure of Calvin's achievement.' *Biographical Dictionary of Evangelicals* (Downers Grove, IL: InterVarsity Press, 2003), 110.

[22] Philip Schaff, *A History of the Christian Church* (New York: Charles Scribner's Sons, 1910), 7:839.

[23] McNeill, *Calvinism*, 185.

[24] The relations between the two men, 'at first united and too soon separated by the religious revolution of the sixteenth century', was 'free, sincere, but tempered with respect'. *Letters of John Calvin*, 39 f. 1.

[25] Calvin treasured his relationship with Theodore Beza, who at Calvin's death continued his ministry in Geneva. When Beza was seriously ill in 1551 Calvin was distraught. He wrote to a friend that Beza was 'a man whose gentle disposition, polished manners, and native candour, had endeared him to all good men. Indeed, I were destitute of human feeling, did I not return the affection of one who loves me with more than a brother's love, and reveres me like a very father.'

3

John Knox's Testimony

The major source for John Knox's testimony is his *History of the Reformation in Scotland*, written between 1559 and 1571.[1] Henry R. Sefton describes this work as 'a remarkable testimony from one of the leading participants in the Reformation movement rather than an objective history, but it is a valuable source of information which all subsequent historians of the period can ignore only at their peril'.[2] W. Stanford Reid quotes W. C. Dickinson who said that in his *History* Knox put 'flesh and blood on the whole Reformation movement'.[3] According to R. M. Healey, Knox's *History* is 'an extended sermon on the duty of Scottish Christians to rely on God'.[4] Jane Dawson writes that the *History of the Reformation in Scotland* 'contains some of the best of Knox's writing, with humour and wit helping him drive home his message'.[5] Knox himself stated that he would 'interlace merriness with earnest matters' in his *History*. David Murison writes that nowhere does Knox 'reveal his own character more fully, warts and all, than in the first and last books of his *History of the Reformation in Scotland*, and whether one approves or not of Knox, it should be remembered that most of the evidence against as well as for him comes from the candour of his own writing'.[6]

In addition to Knox's *History* there are occasional personal comments in his theological writings, and many more in his letters, especially letters to two women, Elizabeth Bowes and Anne Lok, and the recently discovered letters to close friend and colleague Christopher Goodman.

A man of 'the middling sort'.

John Knox was born in Haddington, Scotland, in 1514 or 1515. The Knox family lived in a house on Giffordgate Street, on the banks of the River Tyne.[7] Across the river was the great parish church of St Mary's, known as the 'Lamp of the Lothians', where John Knox was baptized. His father, William, was a farmer or a merchant, perhaps both. John Knox told the Earl of Bothwell that both his grandfathers and his father 'served your Lordship's predecessors, and some of them died under their standards'. Little is known of John Knox's mother, a Sinclair, who may have been related to a more prominent family. Knox simply described himself as of 'the middling sort'.

With Patrick Hamilton 'our history begins'.

The First Book of the *History of the Reformation in Scotland* presents in Knox's words 'the manner and by what persons the light of Christ's evangel has been manifested to this realm'. Knox wrote that it is with the early Protestant Patrick Hamilton that 'our history begins'. For preaching justification by faith in Christ alone, the twenty-four-year-old Hamilton was condemned to die 'by fire for the testimony of God's truth,' wrote Knox.[8] Following Hamilton's martyrdom, Knox recorded that 'the knowledge of God did wondrously increase within this realm, partly by reading, partly by brotherly conference', but chiefly by the work of 'merchants and mariners' importing and distributing Protestant books from the Continent. Satan, however, did not cease, by all means, to maintain his kingdom of darkness, and to suppress the light of Christ's evangel,' Knox wrote.

'I first cast my anchor.'

John Knox studied at the University of St Andrews with one of the foremost teachers of that time, John Major, who had returned to Scotland after a long and distinguished career at the University of Paris. While not sympathetic to the Reformation, Major was openly critical of the abuses of the Roman Catholic Church of his day, and no doubt influenced his students to adopt similar views.

In 1536 Knox was ordained as a priest in the Roman Catholic Church, but was not assigned to a parish. Instead, like both Luther and Calvin, he studied law. He worked for a time as a church notary, drawing up official papers of various kinds. One document Knox notarized was signed

'The faithful witness through Christ, to whom be the glory'—perhaps an indication of his growing Protestant convictions. He abandoned his career in the Church and became a private tutor to several sons of lairds, who were firm supporters of evangelical reform.

Knox does not explain the circumstances of his conversion, but we know he was hearing Protestant preachers and reading the Bible. On his deathbed he asked that someone read the seventeenth chapter of John's Gospel, where, he said, 'I first cast my anchor'. This chapter, writes W. Stanford Reid, 'lays great stress on the Christian's salvation through faith in Christ, calling to Christ's service, the enmity of the world, and assurance of eternal life. These became themes that Knox continuously sounded in his letters, his pamphlets, and his preaching.'[9]

An extract from Knox's lengthy book on *Predestination* may contain a clue about his conversion. In this book he described 'the high-priestly prayer' of Christ in John 17 and wrote: 'O that our hearts could, without contradiction, embrace these words; for then with humility should we prostrate ourselves before our God, and with unfeigned tears give thanks for his mercy! As the love of God the Father was ever constant towards his dear Son, so it is also towards the members of his body; yea even when they are ignorant and enemies unto him, as the apostle Paul witnesses, saying, "God specially commends his love towards us, that when we were yet sinners Christ died for us; much more being justified now by his blood, we shall be saved by him from wrath. For if, when we were enemies, we were reconciled to God by the death of his Son, much more, we, being reconciled, shall be saved by his life.'"

'A man of such graces as before him were never heard within this realm.'

George Wishart was, Knox wrote, 'a man of such graces as before him were never heard within this realm'. In writing about Wishart, Knox mentioned himself for the first time in his *History*. During Wishart's preaching mission in the Lothians, Knox accompanied him as a kind of bodyguard, carrying a great sword. Wishart began his last sermon with the question, 'O Lord, how long shall it be that your holy word shall be despised, and men shall not regard their own salvation?' Wishart knew that he was about to be arrested and persuaded Knox to go home, telling him, 'Return to your bairns and God bless you. One is sufficient for a sacrifice.'[10] Wishart was taken to St Andrews, where, on the orders of Cardinal David Beaton, he was condemned to die for his Protestant beliefs. After celebrating the Lord's Supper with a few friends, Wishart was burned at the stake on March 1, 1546. Just as he had promised, he suffered 'gladly for the word's sake'.[11]

In his *History* Knox recorded a prayer from Wishart, a prayer that Knox made his own: 'O Lord, we know surely that your true servants must suffer, for your name's sake, persecution, affliction, and troubles in this present life, which is but a shadow, as you have shown to us by your prophets and apostles. Yet we desire you, merciful Father, that you would conserve, defend, and help your congregation, which you have chosen before the beginning of the world, and give them your grace to hear your word, and to be your true servants in this present life.'

> *'How small was my learning, and how weak I was of judgment, when Jesus Christ called me to be his steward.'*

A few weeks after Wishart's death, a group of men with mixed motives—political, personal, and religious—murdered Cardinal Beaton and took possession of his castle in St Andrews.[12] Sympathizers joined them, including Knox and his three pupils. Knox wrote: 'At Easter 1547, came to the Castle of St Andrews John Knox, who, wearied of removing from place to place by reason of the persecution that came upon him [by Catholic officials], was determined to have left Scotland, and to have visited the schools of Germany. But he had the care of some gentlemen's children, whom certain years he had nourished in godliness; and their fathers solicited him to go to St Andrews so that he himself might have the benefit of the castle, and their children the benefit of his doctrine.'

When Knox was asked by several of the leaders of the castle to become their preacher, he refused, because, he said, 'he could not run where God had not called him'. After a second call from the entire group, Knox reluctantly accepted. As he wrote about himself in his *History*, 'he, abashed, burst forth in most abundant tears, and withdrew himself to his chamber'. After a few days he went to Holy Trinity Parish Church in the town (at times during the standoff the people in the castle were free to come and go) where he preached his first sermon. Knox said that 'before he began to open the corruptions of the papistry, he defined the true kirk, showed the true notes of it, whereupon it was built, why it was the pillar of verity, and why it could not err, to wit, "Because it heard the voice of its own pastor, Jesus Christ, and would not hear a stranger, neither yet would be carried about with every kind of doctrine."' He then compared 'the doctrine of justification expressed in the Scriptures—which teach that "man is justified by faith only", and that "the blood of Jesus Christ purges us from all our sins"—and the doctrine of the papists, which attributes justification to the works of the law, yea, to the works of man's invention such as pilgrimages, pardons, and such baggage'. Many of his hearers were impressed. They said that 'others cut off the branches of papistry, but he strikes at the root'.

Knox later wrote, 'How small was my learning, and how weak I was of judgment, when Jesus Christ called me to be his steward.' But 'God so assisted his weak soldier and so blessed his labours, that not only all those of the castle, but also a great number of the town of St Andrews, openly professed that same doctrine he taught them.'

'I know how hard the battle is.'

On July 31, 1547, with French ships assisting in the siege, the 'Castilians' were forced to surrender. The gentry were taken as prisoners to France, while the rest, including Knox, were made to work in the galleys of the French fleet. For the next nineteen months he rowed as a galley slave in a 'floating hell'.[13] Knox later wrote in his *Treatise on Prayer* some words that described his experience: 'I know how hard the battle is between the spirit and the flesh, under the heavy cross of affliction, where no worldly defence but present death appears. I know the grudging and murmuring complaints of the flesh; I know the anger, wrath, and indignation which it conceives against God, calling all his promises in doubt, and being ready every hour utterly to fall from God: against which rests only faith, provoking us to call earnestly, and to pray for assistance of God's Spirit. Wherein if we continue, he shall turn our most desperate calamities to gladness, and to a prosperous end.'

Knox, writes W. Stanford Reid, 'seems to have maintained a position of leadership among the Scottish galley slaves, buoyed up by his faith coupled with his sense of humour'.[14] Knox missed his 'congregation of the Castle of St Andrews' and wrote, 'Consider, brethren, it is no speculative theologian who desires to give you courage, but even your brother in affliction.' Knox made at least two trips on the French ships back to St Andrews. When asked if he recognized the port in the distance, Knox, 'extremely sick so that few hoped for his life', replied, 'Yes, I know it well. I see the steeple of that place where God first in public opened my mouth to his glory, and I am fully persuaded, however weak I now appear, that I shall not depart this life till my tongue shall glorify his godly name in that place.'

When Knox was asked by several of his fellow prisoners if they were justified in attempting to escape, he replied that they could do so, but only if they did not 'shed any man's blood for their freedom'. He added, 'I am assured that God will deliver you, but not by such means as you have looked for, that is, by the force of friends or by your own labours.' Knox believed that 'God would so work in the deliverance of them, that the praise thereof should redound to his glory only.'

Knox and the others were released in the spring of 1549, apparently through English negotiations with the French. 'Howsoever it was,' Knox said, 'God made the hearts of their enemies to set them at liberty', adding that God worked powerfully in delivering 'those that had but a small knowledge of his truth, but for the love of the same hazarded all' and that 'the same God that dejects, for causes unknown to us, will raise up again the persons dejected, to his glory and their comfort'.

'God so blessed my weak labours.'

Because it was not safe for him to return to Scotland, Knox went to England, where Archbishop Cranmer was gathering an international group of Protestants to help in the creation of a new Church of England. For five years Knox served churches in the North of England, preached in London, and consulted with those revising the *Book of Common Prayer*.

Knox was appointed pastor of the parish of Berwick-upon-Tweed, a rough border town, and later also served a congregation in Newcastle-upon-Tyne. These two towns gave Knox a place of wide influence in both England and Scotland.

Years later when Mary, Queen of Scots accused Knox of fomenting trouble in the past in England and now in Scotland, Knox told her: 'In England I was resident only the space of five years. The places were Berwick, where I abode two years; so long in Newcastle; and a year in London. Now, Madam, if in any of these places, during the time that I was there, any man shall be able to prove that there was either battle, sedition or mutiny, I shall confess that I myself was the malefactor and shedder of the blood. I am not ashamed, Madam, further to affirm that God so blessed my weak labours that in Berwick (where commonly before there used to be slaughter by reason of quarrels that used to arise amongst soldiers) there was as great quietness all the time that I remained there as there is this day in Edinburgh.'

During his time in England, Knox met two women who became influential in his life, Elizabeth Bowes and Anne Lok.

'A very mirror and glass in which I beheld myself so rightly painted forth.'

Elizabeth Aske Bowes, a married woman from Yorkshire, became a close friend, long-time correspondent, and mother-in-law of John Knox. She was nine years older than the reformer, and when they met she had been married for thirty years and had borne fifteen children. She had accepted the Protestant doctrine of justification by faith alone, probably before Knox's ministry in Berwick began, and maintained her convictions against her family's resistance.

Mrs Bowes had two distinct sides. She was a woman with strong convictions who also struggled with doubts and fears about her own spiritual condition. Again and again she turned to Knox for his counsel. Although sometimes wearied by her constant questions and problems, Knox did his best to help her with a 'mixture of scriptural principles and hard Lowland common sense'.[15] He insisted that her experience was one of the normal trials of true Christians. The saved, Knox wrote to her, 'do not always hear God's word vocally crying to us'. Even Christ on the cross had the feeling of being abandoned by God while in the very act of making 'satisfaction to the justice of God'. Anxiety about one's standing before God, Knox assured Mrs Bowes, was a sign of salvation, because it showed that faith had awakened her to the fact that salvation is 'the free gift of our God, and not proceeding of our works'.

In one of his letters to help dispel her doubts Knox shared the evidence he had of his own salvation: 'The office of the faithful is to keep promises. God promises remission of sins to all that confess the same. I confess my sins for I see the filthiness of them, and how justly God could condemn me for my iniquities. I sob and lament that I cannot be quit and rid of sin. I desire to live a more perfect life. These are infallible signs that God has remitted sin.'

In another letter Knox encouraged Mrs Bowes in words that reflected his own testimony: 'Abide, mother, the time of harvest, before which must needs go the cold of winter, the unstable spring, and the fervent heat of summer. You must sow with tears before you reap with gladness, death before life, weakness before strength, unstableness before stability, and bitterness before comfort.'

In what may have been the first letter Knox wrote to his fiancée, Marjory Bowes, he addressed her as 'Dearly beloved Sister in the common faith of Jesus our Saviour'. More pastoral than personal, the letter included some advice on how Marjory should seek to help with her mother's severe depression. 'The Spirit of God shall instruct your heart about what is most comfortable to the troubled conscience of your mother; pray earnestly that it may be so. When the adversary objects, she ought not to think wicked thoughts; but seeing that our nature is corrupted with sin, which entered by his suggestion, it thinks and works wickedly by his assaults. And when he inquires what Christ is, answer, "He is the seed of the woman promised by God to break down the serpent's head, which he has done already, appearing in our flesh, subject to all passions that may fall in our nature, only sin excepted; and after the death suffered, he has, by power of his Godhead, risen again triumphant victor over death, hell, and sin, not for himself, for thereto was he no debtor, but for those who thirst for salvation by him only, whom he may no more lose, or he would cease to be the Son of God and the Saviour of the world." There is no doubt that Satan, as he is the accuser of all God's elect, studies to trouble her conscience, so that, according to her desire, she may not rest in Jesus our Lord. Be vigilant in prayer.'

When Mrs Bowes wrote that her storm of doubt had for the moment passed but that she felt lethargic and indifferent to her sins, Knox replied that her condition was not unusual. The spirit, like the body, needed periods of rest, as he had learned from his own spiritual struggles. Her troubles and infirmities were, Knox wrote, 'a very mirror and glass in which I beheld myself so rightly painted forth'.

Knox was remarkably frank in his letters to his future mother-in-law. To her he confessed how often he had broken the Ten Commandments: 'I am worse than my pen can express. In body you think I am no adulterer; let so be, but the heart is infected with foul lusts. Externally, I commit no idolatry; but my wicked heart loves itself. I am no man-killer with my hands; but I help not my needy brother so liberally as I may and ought. I steal not horse, money, or clothes from my neighbour; but that small portion of worldly substance I do not so rightly bestow as his holy law requires. I bear no false witness against my neighbour in judgment, or otherwise before men; but I speak not the truth of God so boldly as is fitting for his true messenger to do. And thus in conclusion, there is no vice opposed to God's holy will expressed in his law with which my heart is not infected.'

Knox wrote that his words to Mrs Bowes were 'more plain than ever I spoke' and were written to let her know that she had a 'companion in trouble'. Furthermore, Knox found that her questions and doubts caused him to prove the meaning of Scripture more deeply than he would have done on his own. She brought out in Knox qualities of humility and sympathy that helped balance his strength and vigour.

In his *Exposition of the Sixth Psalm*, dedicated to Mrs Bowes, Knox wrote: 'What boldness I have seen in you in all such conflicts, it needs not me to rehearse. I write this to the praise of God; I have wondered at that bold constancy which I have found in you at such a time as my own heart was faint. Sure I am that flesh and blood could never have persuaded you to have despised and counted as nothing those things which the world most esteems. You have tasted and felt of God's goodness and mercy in such measure that not only are you able to reason and speak, but also, by the Spirit of God working in you, to give comfort and consolation to such as were in trouble.'

'I have rather need of all than that any has need of me.'

Anne Vaughan Lok[16] was 'a prominent, active, and articulate member of the English Reformed community'. She was raised in a family with substantial financial and political connections, and which supported the Protestant reform movement. Knox met Anne Lok, young wife of a merchant in London, in 1552. He apparently stayed with Anne and Henry Lok and the family of Henry Lok's half-sister, Rose Hickman, during the winter of 1552–53 before his departure for the Continent. Knox wrote that Anne Lok and Rose Hickman were kind to him 'with a special care over me, as the mother uses over her natural child'. They were 'more dear to him than all in London', and he was assured of their 'constant love and care'. Later he urged Mrs Lok and Mrs Hickman to leave London, with its dangers to Protestants and its temptations to compromise their convictions, and to join him in Geneva. In 1557, as persecution increased, Mrs Lok, with her two children and her maid, left England for

Geneva, where Knox was serving as pastor of the church of English exiles. A learned and talented woman, Mrs Lok translated Calvin's sermons on the Song of Hezekiah, which she published along with a poetic meditation of her own on Psalm 51.

Like Elizabeth Bowes, Anne Lok corresponded with Knox about her spiritual questions. He responded sympathetically, encouraging her to trust what she already knew to be true. He reminded her to wrestle with God, as Jacob did with the angel, and assured her 'that you are not destitute of his Holy Spirit, for it flows and gives witness of itself in your grievous complaint and earnest prayer'. In a letter to Mrs Lok, after she returned to England, Knox answered her concerns about her relationship to the Church of England: 'Neither my pen, nor yet my presence, can prescribe to you how far you are indebted to expose yourself to dangers from these imperfections in religion that you cannot remedy. But you, directing your heart to advance God's glory, shall be instructed by his Holy Spirit as to how far you may condescend and how far you are bound to abstain.'

As he did with Mrs Bowes, Knox shared with Mrs Lok some of his own struggles. He admitted that he was by nature 'churlish', but that he needed and valued his friends. 'The cause may be,' he wrote, 'that I have rather need of all than that any has need of me.'

Anne Lok 'was a strong woman, dedicated to the Protestant cause and actively loyal to it throughout her life'.[17]

Knox valued her friendship and honoured her as a colleague in the work of the Reformation.

'It is not Christ's presence in the bread that can save us, but his presence in our hearts through faith in his blood.'

While he was ministering in the North of England, Knox was ordered to defend his sharp criticism of the Roman Catholic Mass before a large congregation at the parish church of Newcastle. Knox insisted that 'the sacrifice of the Mass is idolatry', and that 'it is not Christ's presence in the bread that can save us, but his presence in our hearts through faith in his blood, which has washed out our sins, and pacified his Father's wrath toward us'. His uncompromising presentation ended with some personal words of testimony: 'And here I call my God to record that neither profit to myself, hatred of any person or persons, nor affection or favour that I bear towards any private man, causes me this day to speak as you have heard; but only the obedience that I owe to God in the ministry, showing of his word, and the common love which I bear to the salvation of all men.'

Knox was not suspected of using his ministry to profit himself. Even Knox's bitterest enemies never accused him of seeking wealth or position by his reforming ministry. *The Catholic Encyclopedia* admits that 'it is to Knox's credit that he died, as he had lived, a poor man, and that he never enriched himself with the spoils of the church which he had abandoned'.[18] Neither can Knox be accused of flattery. Standing beside Knox's open grave, the Earl of Morton uttered words long remembered: 'Here lies one who never feared nor flattered any flesh.'

Knox also said that he did not hate any person. He does, at times, speak of his hatred, but to him it was like the 'holy hatred' expressed by the writers of the Psalms against God's enemies, and therefore the enemies of the Reformation, especially the three Marys—Mary Tudor of England, Mary Guise of France, and Mary, Queen of Scots. Writing from France to his 'afflicted brethren' in England in 1554, Knox cautioned them not to have 'a carnal hatred' towards their Roman Catholic persecutors but to pray for their repentance: 'Beloved brethren, you must avoid two things. The former, that you do not presume to be revengers of your own cause, but that you resign vengeance to him who only is able to requite them, according to their malicious minds. Secondly, that you do not hate with any carnal hatred these blind, cruel, and malicious tyrants; but that you learn of Christ to pray for your persecutors, lamenting and bewailing that the devil should so prevail against them that headlong they should run, body and soul, to perpetual perdition. And note well what I say, we may not hate them with a carnal hatred: that is to say, only because they trouble our bodies—for there is a spiritual hatred, which David calls a perfect hatred, which the Holy Ghost engenders in the hearts of God's elect against the rebellious despisers of his holy statutes.'

'Thus did light and darkness strive within the realm of Scotland'—and England.

After four years in the North, Knox was called to the South of England. He was appointed one of six chaplains to King Edward VI, preaching before the king and court on occasion and travelling widely to promote the cause of the Reformation. In his *History* Knox makes no mention of his appointment as a royal chaplain, nor the invitations he received to prominent posts, including the bishopric of Rochester and the living of All Hallows in London.

Knox had heard about Christopher Goodman, but they did not meet until the start of Mary Tudor's reign. Years later Knox reminded Goodman of how they had walked on the city walls at Chester, and had discussed whether to flee from the Roman Catholic rule then being re-established in England under Mary. Knox urged Goodman not to remain 'within Satan's bloody claws', believing that God would keep him 'for another time to the great comfort of his church'. Christopher Goodman remained a close friend and valued colleague of Knox in England, Frankfurt, Geneva, and Scotland.[19]

In his *History* Knox described how 'light and darkness' did strive 'within the realm of Scotland from the death of that notable servant of God, Master Patrick Hamilton, to the death of Edward the Sixth, the most godly and most virtuous king that has been known to reign in England'. The religious situation in England changed dramatically under Mary Tudor, known in history as 'Bloody Mary'. For a few months Knox continued to preach in various places in England, often to large gatherings drawn together by his popularity and the looming crisis.

'My prayer is that I may be restored to the battle again.'

As the direction of Mary Tudor's reign became clear, and danger to outspoken Protestants like Knox increased, he and many others left England for the safety of the Continent. Knox looked back with some misgivings that he had to leave England. 'And although I have, in the beginning of this battle, appeared to play the faint-hearted and feeble soldier, my prayer is that I may be restored to the battle again. Blessed be God the Father of our Lord Jesus Christ, who never despises the sobs of the sore afflicted. Through him I shall be encouraged to fight so that England and Scotland shall both know that I am ready to suffer more than either poverty or exile for the profession of that doctrine and that heavenly religion of which it has pleased his merciful providence to make me, among others, a simple soldier and witness bearer to men.'

From France Knox wrote to Mrs Bowes ('dear mother', he now called her) assuring her that there were those in

France who would look after his needs, but if people failed to help him, 'God will send his ravens; so that, in every place, perhaps I may find some feathers to cover my body'. He added, 'But, alas, where I shall find children to be begotten to God by the word of life, that I cannot presently consider. The spiritual life of such as sometimes boldly professed Christ, God knows is to my heart more dear than all the glory, riches, and honour on earth.'

Knox could no longer preach to his English congregations, but he prayed for them and wrote to them long, sermon-like letters that also contained personal comments. Knox said that the troubles in England were more sorrowful to him than even the troubles in Scotland.

In France he completed and published his *Treatise on Prayer*, to instruct and encourage 'the small and dispersed flock of Jesus Christ' in England to trust God in uncertain times. He described what true prayer is, how we should pray, and for what we should pray. He wrote that Christians should 'offer to God most humble obedience' in all our afflictions, for we know not what to ask or desire as we ought. Our 'frail flesh, oppressed with fear and pain, desires deliverance, ever abhorring and drawing back from giving obedience'. He added, 'O Christian brethren, I write by experience.'

'Your blessed gospel was in our ears like a lover's song.'

Knox wrote *A Godly Letter of Warning or Admonition to the Faithful in London, Newcastle and Berwick* to encourage and instruct the believers in those places that he had served. They must at all costs avoid idolatry, which Knox described as doing anything contrary to God's word, and practice forbearance, patience, and hope. He wrote: 'Mark, brethren, that many make an idol of their own wisdom or fantasy, more trusting to that which they think good' than that which the 'Lord God has commanded them'.

There followed *Two Comfortable Epistles to His Afflicted Brethren in England*. He wrote: 'For yet my good hope is that one day or other Christ Jesus, who now in England is crucified, shall rise again in spite of his enemies, and shall appear to his weak and sorely troubled disciples, to whom he shall say, "Peace be unto you. It is I; fear not."'

In his lengthy *Faithful Admonition to the Professors of God's Truth in England*, Knox reflected on the window of opportunity for the gospel now suddenly closed and drew lessons from it for himself and for his brothers and sisters still in England. He was especially aware of his own faults. 'We the ministers, who were the distributors of this bread (the true word of God) by which the multitude within England was fed, did not lack our offences, which also moved God to send us to the sea. And because the offences of no man are so clear to me as my own, I will accuse only myself.'

Knox described the bold confidence of Peter and his subsequent failure and no doubt applied to himself what God taught the apostle. 'But to correct and inform both presumptuous arrogance and frail imbecility and weakness of faith, Peter was permitted once to sink, and thrice most shamefully to refuse and deny his Master; to the intent that by the knowledge of his own weakness, he might be more able to instruct others of the same; and also that he might more largely magnify God's free grace and mighty deliverance. Christ taught him before his falling, saying, "When you are converted, strengthen your brethren", as though Christ should have said, "Peter, you are yet too proud to be a pastor. You do not stoop, nor bow your back down to take up the weak sheep. You do not yet know your own infirmity and weakness, and therefore you can do nothing but despise the weak ones. But when you shall be instructed by experience about your own self what hidden iniquity lurks within the nature of man, then shall you learn to be humble and stoop among other sinners. And also you shall be an example to others, who shall offend as you did. So that if they repent as you did, they need not despair of mercy, but may trust most assuredly in Christ to obtain grace, mercy, and forgiveness, as you did.'

In his *Faithful Admonition* Knox included this prayer of confession for himself and his English friends: 'We acknowledge and confess, O Lord, that we are punished most justly, because we lightly regarded the time of our merciful visitation. Your blessed gospel was in our ears like a lover's song, pleasing us for a time; but alas! our lives did not agree with your statutes and holy commandments. And thus we acknowledge that our iniquity has compelled your justice to take the light of your word from the whole realm of England.'

'I could wish my name to perish so that God's book and glory might only be sought among us.'

In his *History of the Reformation in Scotland* Knox passed over his ministry on the Continent in a few sentences: 'When he left England he then passed to Geneva, and there remained in private study till he was called by the English congregation, then assembled at Frankfurt, to be preacher to them. Which vocation he obeyed, albeit unwillingly, at the commandment of that notable servant of God, John Calvin. At Frankfurt he remained, till some of the learned, whose names we suppress, more given to unprofitable ceremonies than to sincerity of religion, began to quarrel with the said John [Knox]. They accused him of treason committed against the Emperor Charles V, and against their Sovereign, Queen Mary of England, because in his *Admonition to England*, he called the one little inferior to Nero, and the other more cruel than Jezebel. So the said John [Knox] returned to Geneva, from there to Dieppe, and thereafter to Scotland.'

From France, Knox travelled to Switzerland to seek advice from Calvin, Viret, and Bullinger. He was impressed by Calvin and Geneva, and he decided to settle there to study and prepare for his return to England or Scotland in due course.

Several months into his studies in Geneva, Knox was invited to become a minister of a church of English exiles in Frankfurt. With Calvin's blessing he went to Frankfurt, where he became involved in controversy concerning the form of worship the church was to follow. Some of the congregation wanted to follow strictly the English *Book of Common Prayer*, but Knox wanted to make some changes to reflect the Genevan liturgy. 'I could wish my name to perish,' Knox said, 'so that God's book and glory might only be sought among us.' Despite Knox's suggestion of a composite liturgy, his opponents prevailed, and he sadly but wisely made his way back to Geneva. Christopher Goodman stayed on for a time as leader of the 'Knoxian' party, but soon led a group of English exiles to Geneva.

'The most perfect school of Christ.'

In Geneva Knox found, to his delight, a Reformed church with confession, worship, and discipline carefully drawn from the word of God. It was 'the most perfect school of Christ that ever was in the earth since the days of the apostles,' Knox wrote. 'In other places, I confess Christ to be truly preached; but manners and religion so sincerely reformed, I have not yet seen in any other place.' Because of its peacefulness, after England and Frankfurt, Knox humorously referred to Geneva as 'a den of ease'.

The remarkable English community in Geneva was busy producing the essential tools for a Reformed church in England—a new translation of the Bible, a metrical psalter, and a revised liturgy. Knox was busy writing and studying. He wrote to Anne Lok informing her that his letters were no longer so extensive because the demands upon him 'do compel me often to forget not only my most special friends, but also myself'.

'If I had not seen it with my eyes in my own country, I could not have believed it.'

Knox was happy in Geneva but he could not forget Scotland. He travelled to Scotland in 1555 and married Marjory Bowes. He also sought to further the cause of the Reformation in his homeland. During a short, busy preaching tour he met with the leaders of the Protestant movement and administered the Lord's Supper in the homes of his supporters.[20] It was Marjory's mother, Knox wrote, whom God had used to draw him from his 'rest of quiet study to see and contemplate the fervent thirst of our brethren, night and day sobbing and groaning for the bread of life. If I had not seen it with my eyes in my own country, I could not have believed it.'

While in Scotland, Knox preached a sermon on the temptations of Christ in the wilderness. He sent a copy to Mrs Lok, reporting that some who were 'in great anguish' said that they were 'somewhat reclaimed' by it. In Edinburgh Knox met a woman with 'a troubled conscience', who said that he 'opened more fully the fountain of God's mercy' to her than anyone she had heard preach. She died not long after with a ringing testimony of God's blessing. Knox wrote in his *History* that he 'could not omit this worthy woman who gave so notable a confession before the great light of God's word did universally shine' in Scotland.

Roman Catholic prelates, alarmed by the success of Knox's preaching, summoned him to appear before them in Edinburgh. When Knox arrived with a large company of Protestant supporters, the Roman Catholics backed off. On the day of the cancelled meeting, Knox preached to a larger congregation than he had yet addressed in the nation's capital. He sent a letter to Mary, the queen regent, asking her to show 'motherly pity' to her evangelical subjects and to allow Protestant preachers freedom to carry on their work. The regent flippantly dismissed the letter as a joke.

While in Scotland, Knox received a letter from the English church in Geneva asking him to return as their pastor. Knox's *History* states that 'upon which the said John [Knox] took his leave from us, and, almost in every congregation where he had preached, exhorted us to prayer, to reading the Scriptures, and mutual conference, until such a time as God should give us greater liberty'.

After Knox departed for Geneva, the Roman Catholic authorities tried him *in absentia*, condemned him, and burned him in effigy. Knox published an enlarged version of his letter to the queen regent claiming that the bishops 'against all justice and equity have pronounced against me a most cruel sentence, condemning my body to fire, my soul to damnation, and all doctrine taught by me to be false, deceitful, and heretical'.

'A Letter of Wholesome Counsel to His Brethren in Scotland.'

Before leaving Scotland, Knox wrote *A Letter of Wholesome Counsel to His Brethren in Scotland,* not so much to instruct them, he wrote, but 'to leave with them some testimony of my love'. He encouraged them to be 'frequent in the law of your Lord God', advising them to read the Old Testament along with the New Testament, 'for it shall greatly comfort you to hear that harmony and well-tuned song of the Holy Spirit speaking in our fathers from the beginning'. He wrote that St Paul calls the gospel 'the sweet odour of life to those that shall receive life, borrowing a similitude of odoriferous herbs or precious ointments, whose nature is that the more they be touched or moved, the more they send forth their odour more pleasant and delectable: even such, dear brethren, is the blessed evangel of our Lord Jesus;

for the more that it be entreated, the more comfortable and powerful it is to such as do hear, read, or exercise it.'

In his *Letter* Knox instructed that worship be observed in every household at least once a day, with reading and discussion of Scripture, as well as prayer. He described public worship: 'Your assemblies ought to begin with confession and invocation of God's Holy Spirit, and finish with thanksgiving and common prayers for princes, rulers, and magistrates; for the liberty and free passage of Christ's evangel, for the comfort and deliverance of our afflicted brethren in all places now persecuted, but most cruelly within the realm of France and England; and for such other things as the Spirit of the Lord Jesus shall teach to be profitable, either to yourselves or to your brethren wherever they be.'

'The most delightful of wives.'

Knox returned to Geneva with his bride, Marjory, and his mother-in-law, Mrs Bowes, who left her husband and the rest of her family to accompany Knox and her daughter. Calvin called Marjory 'the most delightful of wives', and told Knox that she was 'a rare find'. Despite many cares and concerns, Knox now entered the happiest period of his life.

Jane Dawson begins her biography of the Scottish reformer thus: 'It was a Sunday [May 23, 1557] not like any other Sunday in John Knox's life. As the afternoon sermon came to an end, Knox was standing beneath the pulpit proudly cradling his newborn son in his arms. Being a man to whom tears came easily, he was probably weeping with happiness. At his shoulder was his close friend William Whittingham, who had supported him through thick and thin in the recent troubles at Frankfurt, and was standing godfather … to him and his son. The minister, Christopher Goodman, Whittingham's friend since childhood, came down from the pulpit after preaching the sermon. These three men of such different temperaments had forged a deep friendship at Frankfurt, and now in Geneva Knox and Goodman served as co-ministers to this church for English-speaking exiles, while Whittingham organized the congregation's great biblical translation project. They had all been involved in writing the service of baptism that was about to begin.'[21]

'The First Blast of the Trumpet.'

In Geneva Knox wrote and published his most famous (or infamous) treatise, *The First Blast of the Trumpet Against the Monstrous Regiment of Women*, 'thus committing one of his greatest political blunders'.[22] Knox argued that female rule was contrary to the rational arguments of the philosophers and the mandate of Scripture. He called for an English uprising to remove Mary Tudor, advocating the right of resistance to an ungodly ruler, a view that shocked most of his contemporaries.

'The *First Blast* was intended to be the first of three,' writes C. S. Lewis, 'but it was loud enough alone.'[23] While the treatise was aimed at Mary Tudor of England and Mary of Guise, the regent for Mary, Queen of Scots, it came out just in time to greatly offend the English and Protestant Queen Elizabeth. Knox acknowledged that his *First Blast* blew away all his friends in England. One important friend who did not agree with Knox but continued to support him was William Cecil, Queen Elizabeth's Secretary of State and Knox's most influential ally in England. Cecil began a letter to Knox with a cautious rebuke: 'There is neither male nor female; for, as saith Paul, they are all one in Christ Jesus. Blessed is the man who trusteth in the Lord; the Lord will be his confidence.'

Knox spent the rest of his life defending, explaining, adjusting, even criticizing his *First Blast* with little success. In a brief summary of his proposed *Second Blast of the Trumpet* Knox did not mention women at all but states forthrightly that a 'manifestly wicked' ruler may be deposed and punished—the point he wanted to make all along!

'In the hope of the life to come he has made all equal.'

In 1557 Knox decided, in response to an urgent request from Scottish nobles and with Calvin's encouragement, to visit Scotland once again. When he arrived at the French port of Dieppe, however, letters from Scotland awaited him, advising him to delay his coming until a more favourable time. Knox wrote to the Scottish nobles, chiding them for their faint-heartedness and expressing his dismay at being compelled to leave Geneva without accomplishing anything: 'To some it may appear a small and light matter that I have cast off, and as it were abandoned as well, my particular care, as my public office and charge, leaving my house and poor family destitute of all head, save God only, and committing that small (but to Christ dearly beloved) flock, over which I was appointed one of the ministers, to the charge of another.'

Knox admitted that his words to the nobles might appear to some sharp and indiscreetly spoken, but insisted that 'as charity ought to interpret all things to the best, so ought wise men to understand that a true friend cannot be a flatterer, especially when the question of salvation, both of body and soul, is moved'. Knox ended his letter with the benediction, 'The Mighty Spirit of the Lord Jesus rule and guide your counsels to his glory, your eternal comfort, and consolation of your brethren.'

Knox wrote a warm and encouraging letter to 'the Commonalty of Scotland', filled with scriptural promises and exhorting the people to understand that 'the reformation and care of religion' was just as much their task as it was the responsibility of the nobles: 'Beloved brethren, you are God's creatures, created and formed in his own image and likeness, for whose redemption was shed the most precious blood of the only beloved Son of God. To you he has commanded his gospel and glad tidings to be preached, and for whom he has prepared a heavenly inheritance, so that you will not obstinately refuse and disdainfully despise the means, his blessed evangel, which now he offers to you, to the end that you may be saved. For the gospel and glad tidings of the kingdom truly preached is the power of God to the salvation of every believer. It is for you, the Commonalty, no less than for your rulers and princes. For albeit God has put and ordained distinction and difference between the rulers and the common people in the government and administration of civil policies, yet in the hope of the life to come he has made all equal.'

'We shall faithfully declare what moved us to put our hands to the reformation of religion.'

Knox introduced the second book of his *History*, covering the years 1558 and 1559, with these words: 'In this our confession, we shall faithfully declare what moved us to put our hands to the reformation of religion, to the end that, our cause being known, both our enemies and our brethren in all realms may understand how falsely we are accused of tumult and rebellion, and how unjustly we are persecuted by France and their faction. Also that our brethren, natural Scotsmen, of whatever religion they be, may have occasion to examine themselves, whether they may with safe conscience oppose themselves to us, who seek nothing but Christ Jesus to be preached; his holy sacraments to be truly administered; superstition, tyranny, and idolatry to be suppressed in this realm; and finally, the liberty of this our native country to remain free from the bondage and tyranny of strangers.'

Knox freed himself from some of the doctrines and many of the practices of the Roman Catholic Church of his time, but not from the intolerance of that church which by statement and action attempted to suppress all 'heresies' by fire and sword. Like the Roman Catholics Knox believed that there could be only one church in Scotland. Although at times Knox insisted that Protestant rulers and people fight to establish and maintain the Reformed church, and only the Reformed church, in Scotland, he knew and believed that the church would exist only by the winning of the minds and hearts of the Scottish people to the Reformed faith. To the Roman Catholic persecutors of the Protestants, Knox said, 'God will not use his saints and chosen children to punish you. With them is always mercy, even though God has pronounced a curse. He will punish you by those in whom there is no mercy.'

Knox denounced sharply, and sometimes harshly, his opponents (or, as he would say, 'God's enemies') but he did not assign them to perdition as the Roman Catholics did. When the Roman Catholic Bishop of Orkney was poisoned early in 1558, Knox, telling the story in his *History*, wrote that the Protestant Lord James, later Earl of Moray, came to visit the bishop. Lord James exhorted him 'to call to mind the promises of God and the virtue of Christ's death'. The bishop answered, 'Nay, my Lord, let me alone. You and I never agreed in our life, and I think we shall not agree now at my death.' Knox commented, 'The Lord James departed to his lodging, and the other shortly after departed this life; whither the great day of the Lord will declare!'

Pray that I would 'shrink not when the battle approaches'.

After five years on the Continent, Knox returned to Scotland for good in 1559. He set off for Dieppe on January 28, leaving Marjory and her mother behind in Geneva in the care of close friends. From Dieppe he sent a request to William Cecil, Queen Elizabeth's Secretary of State, for permission to enter and travel through England. While he waited for her answer, he served the Huguenot community in Dieppe. Queen Elizabeth, stung by Knox's *First Blast*, refused to allow him entry to England. Knox then took ship directly to Scotland, determined by life or by death to further the cause of the Reformation there. He wrote to Anne Lok, asking her to pray that he would 'shrink not when the battle approaches'.

'We sought to have the face of a church among us.'

John Knox arrived in Scotland on May 2, and a few days later preached in Dundee the first of a notable succession of sermons. In Perth, after a sermon on Christ cleansing the temple, images in the parish church were destroyed by what Knox later called 'the rascal multitude'. Knox did not encourage the destruction of Roman Catholic buildings and images, but his sermons inflamed the passions of others who had no qualms about vandalism. Knox attempted 'to stay the fury of the multitude', he wrote, but confessed that he was not able 'to put order universally'. In a sermon preached at Stirling, he exhorted the people 'to amendment of life, to prayers, and to the works of charity'. Knox explained in a letter to Sir Henry Percy, 'We mean neither sedition, neither yet rebellion against any just and lawful authority, but only the advancement of Christ's religion and the liberty of this poor realm.'[24]

'This our weak beginning,' Knox wrote, 'God did so bless that within a few months the hearts of many were so strengthened that we sought to have the face of a church among us, and open crimes to be punished without respect of persons.'

'My life is in the custody of him whose glory I seek.'

After several years of relative tolerance, Mary of Guise decided to confront the growing Protestant movement. Knox at first hoped that the queen regent would prove supportive of the Reformation. In his *History* he wrote that he held a 'good opinion of her sincerity', and in a letter to Calvin praised her 'for excellent knowledge in God's word, and good will towards the advancement of his glory'. Before long, however, Knox realized that she did not intend to keep her word. The result was civil war.

In St Andrews, Knox preached before Protestant leaders, Catholic prelates, and common folk, choosing again as his text the relevant story of Christ cleansing the temple.[25] He began: 'In this town and church began God first to call me to the dignity of a preacher, from which I was reft by the tyranny of France and by procurement of the bishops, as you all know. How long I continued prisoner, what torment I sustained in the galleys, and what were the sobs of my heart, is now no time to recite. This only I cannot conceal, which more than one has heard me say when the body was far absent from Scotland, that my assured hope was, in open audience, to preach in St Andrews before I departed this life.'

Hearers took the wooden statues and furnishings of the church to the place where the aged Protestant preacher Walter Myln had been executed the previous year and symbolically burned them on that spot.

Encouraged, Knox wrote to Anne Lok: 'The long thirst of my wretched heart is satisfied in abundance, that is, above my expectation, for now forty days and more has my God used my tongue in my native country to his glory. The thirst of the poor people, as well as of the nobility here, is wondrous great, which puts me in comfort that Christ Jesus shall triumph for a space, here in the North and extreme parts of the earth.'

Knox knew, however, that he faced danger and possibly death. He told the Roman Catholic authorities who were determined to prevent his preaching, 'My life is in the custody of him whose glory I seek. I desire the hand or weapon of no man to defend me. Only do I crave audience. Which, if it be denied me at this time, I must seek further where I may have it.' Whatever the cost, he had to preach.

'We do nothing but go about Jericho, blowing with trumpets as God gives strength.'

In June of 1559, the army of the Protestant leaders (who were known as the Lords of the Congregation) occupied Edinburgh, and John Knox was called to be minister at St Giles' on July 7. The city was tense and dangerous. Knox wrote that he hardly had four hours' sleep in twenty-four and was writing 'with sleeping eyes'. He was hoping to get a good horse, 'for great watch is laid for my apprehension, and large money promised to anyone who would kill me'.

In the face of fierce opposition, the Reformation movement began to prevail. Knox gave all the credit to God. He wrote to Anne Lok, 'We do nothing but go about Jericho, blowing with trumpets as God gives strength, hoping victory by his power alone.' Knox's blowing of the trumpet was effective. Thomas Randolph, Queen Elizabeth's ambassador to Scotland, said that the voice of Knox was 'able in one hour to put more life in us than 500 trumpets continuously blasting in our ears'.

In Geneva Calvin heard of the astonishing success of the gospel in Scotland. He wrote to Knox: 'It was a source of pleasure, not to me only but to all pious persons to whom

I communicated the agreeable tidings, to hear of the very great success which has crowned your labours. But as we are astonished at such incredible progress in so brief a space of time, so we likewise give thanks to God whose singular blessing is signally displayed herein.'

> *'We have had wonderful experience*
> *of God's merciful providence.'*

But victory was not yet won. St Andrews became the eastern headquarters for the Protestants, and Knox was based there during most of the fighting of 1559–60. Marjory and her mother came from Geneva. Knox's friend Christopher Goodman became minister, first at Ayr, and then at St Andrews to serve the congregation there while Knox travelled as an army chaplain.

When French soldiers defeated the Scottish Protestants in several towns of Fife, the queen regent exulted, 'Where is now John Knox's God? My God is now stronger than his— yes, even in Fife!' Knox encouraged the Protestants with 'a most comfortable sermon' about the danger in which the disciples of Christ Jesus found themselves when they were in the midst of the sea and Jesus was on the mountain. 'Abide a little!' Knox said. 'The boat shall be saved; and Peter, who had left the boat, shall not drown. God grant that you may acknowledge his hand, after your eyes have seen his deliverance.'

Despite her dislike of Knox, the English Queen Elizabeth, fearing a French victory north of the border, began
to send help to the Scottish Protestants. The sighting of
English ships in the Firth of Forth in January 1560 was the
turning point in the war. That event, writes Reid, 'seemed
to indicate that Knox's God was still in control'.[26] Knox
wrote to Anne Lok, 'We have had wonderful experience of
God's merciful providence; and, for my own part, I were
more than unthankful if I should not confess that God has
heard the sobs of my wretched heart, and has not deceived
me of that little sparkle of hope which his Holy Spirit did
kindle and foster in my heart.' He urged her to appeal to
the faithful in London to help support the Protestant cause
in Scotland by contributing money, which he felt would be
a true demonstration of Christian charity. He concluded
with a request that she obtain for him Calvin's *Commentary
on Isaiah* (recently republished with a dedication to Queen
Elizabeth) and the new edition of Calvin's *Institutes*, and
'any other books that be new and profitable'. Knox added
that in light of the troubles coming to his 'afflicted flock' in
Scotland, it was better to sigh and complain before God, so
that one was forced to run to Jesus, than to succumb to 'the
opinion of virtue that puffs up our pride'.

'We beseech you never to suffer us to forsake or deny this your verity which now we profess.'

Knox's fiery sermons at St Giles' proved something of a problem for the Lords of the Congregation, who arranged for him to go to St Andrews on January 29, 1560. Knox wrote, 'I am judged among ourselves too extreme', and therefore 'I have extracted myself from all public assemblies to my private study'.

Knox did not stay in St Andrews long. In June 1560 the queen regent unexpectedly died. Knox described in his *History* the death of Mary of Guise, reporting that a minister was sent to her who 'did plainly show to her as well the virtue and strength of the death of Jesus Christ as the vanity and abomination of that idol the Mass'. 'She did openly confess,' wrote Knox, 'that there was no salvation but in and by the death of Jesus Christ.' But Knox could not forget her insistence that 'the preachers of Jesus Christ should either die or be banished' from Scotland. Knox stated that in her death 'Christ Jesus got no small victory over such an enemy.'

There was a thanksgiving service in St Giles', no doubt conducted by Knox, who prayed:

'Oh, give us hearts with reverence and fear, to meditate on your wondrous works late wrought in our eyes. We beseech you, O Father of mercies, that as of your undeserved grace you have partly removed our darkness, suppressed idolatry, and taken from above our heads the devouring sword of merciless strangers, so it would please you to proceed with us in this your grace begun. And albeit that in us there is nothing that may move your majesty to show us your favour, yet for Christ Jesus' sake, we beseech you never to suffer us to forsake or deny this your truth which now we profess.

'Give us your grace to live in that Christian charity that your Son, our Lord Jesus, has so earnestly commanded to all members of his body; so that other nations, provoked by our example, may set aside all ungodly war, contention, and strife, and study to live in tranquillity and peace, as becomes the sheep of your pasture, and the people that daily look for our final deliverance by the coming again of our Lord Jesus. To whom, with you, and the Holy Spirit be all honour, glory, and praise, now and ever. Amen.'

'Long have we thirsted, dear brethren, to have made known to the world the doctrine which we profess.'

Knox resumed his position as minister of St Giles', preaching to great numbers of people on the book of Haggai, the prophet who had called upon the people of Israel recently returned from exile to build the house of God before turning their attention to their own houses. 'The doctrine was proper for the time,' Knox wrote, but not everyone was happy with his sermons. 'Some, having greater respect to the world than to God's glory, feeling themselves pricked, said mockingly, "We must now forget ourselves, and bear the barrow to build the houses of God."'

In July 1560 the foreign troops withdrew from Scotland: the French sailed away, and the English army marched for home. Knox led a service of thanksgiving in St Giles' Kirk, remembering in his fervent prayer 'our confederates of England, the instruments by whom we are now set at liberty'.

The 'Reformation Parliament', as it came to be known, opened on the first day of August and faced the daunting task of creating a new Reformed church for Scotland. Knox and five other ministers, all with the first name of 'John', drew up a *Confession of Faith* in four days. It begins with words written by Knox or influenced and approved by him: 'Long have we thirsted, dear brethren, to have made known to the world the doctrine which we profess and for which we have suffered abuse and danger: but such has been the rage of Satan against us, and against the eternal truth of Christ now recently reborn among us, that until this day we have had neither time nor opportunity to set forth our faith, as gladly we would have done. For how we have been afflicted until now the greater part of Europe, we suppose, knows well.'

The *Confession* closes: 'Arise, O Lord, and let your enemies be confounded; let them flee from your presence that hate your godly name. Give your servants strength to speak your word with boldness, and let all nations cleave to the true knowledge of you. Amen.' With these words, gathered from Psalm 68:2 and Acts 4:29, the *Confession* ends as it begins with prayer for the worldwide spread of the gospel.

With little or no violence, far-reaching reforms were promptly enacted. The celebration of the Mass and papal authority throughout the land were abolished. The *Geneva Bible*, with copious marginal notes, appeared, translated and produced in Geneva by Knox's friends. The *First Book of Discipline*, showing the unmistakable mark of Knox's genius and vision, set forth the Presbyterian form of church government, organized a system of universal free education, provided for the support of ministers and ministerial students, and urged every church to help the poor, 'whom not only God the Father in his law, but Christ in his evangel, and the Holy Spirit speaking by St Paul, has so earnestly commended to our care'.

> *I am 'called of my God to instruct the ignorant, comfort the sorrowful, confirm the weak, and rebuke the proud'.*

The first meeting of the General Assembly of the new Church of Scotland met in Edinburgh in December 1560. Knox was not chosen as one of the superintendents (probably his own desire), but happily gave the exhortation for the Superintendent of Lothian. Knox's words reveal his understanding of what it means to be a minister of the gospel, and so they form an important part of his testimony. 'Take heed to yourself, and to the flock committed to your charge;

feed the same carefully, not as it were of compulsion, but of very love, which you bear to the Lord Jesus. Walk in simplicity and pureness of life, as it becomes the true servant and ambassador of the Lord Jesus. Usurp not dominion nor tyrannical empire over your brethren. Be not discouraged in adversity, but lay before yourself the example of prophets, apostles, and of the Lord Jesus, who in their ministry sustained contradiction, contempt, persecution and death. Fear not to rebuke the world of sin, justice, and judgment. If anything succeed prosperously in your vocation, be not puffed up with pride; neither yet flatter yourself as if the good success proceeded from your virtue, industry, or care: but let ever that sentence of the apostle remain in your heart: "What have you, which you have not received? If you have received, why do you glory?" Comfort the afflicted, support the poor, and exhort others to support them. Be not solicitous for the things of this life, but be fervent in prayer to God for increase of his Holy Spirit. And finally, behave yourself in this holy vocation with such sobriety that God may be glorified in your ministry: and so you shall shortly obtain the victory and receive the crown promised, when the Lord Jesus shall appear in his glory, whose omnipotent Spirit assist you and us to the end. Amen.'

Knox happily turned to what he considered his primary work, the preaching of the gospel. In the preface to a sermon on Isaiah 26, Knox wrote (in what David F. Wright called 'an important autobiographical fragment') that he thought himself 'rather called of my God to instruct the ignorant, comfort the sorrowful, confirm the weak, and rebuke the proud, by tongue and lively voice in these most corrupt days, than to compose books for the age to come'. Knox was thankful that God had been pleased 'in his mercy' to make him 'not a lord-like bishop, but a painful preacher of his blessed evangel'. Wright states that for Knox, the Bible was more than 'a scholarly, literary text'. It was 'the flaming and searing sword of the Spirit, wielded in living combat for the souls of men and women and for the heart of the church'.[27]

'Dearest spouse of blessed memory.'

Marjory Knox died in December 1560. Her husband mourned her loss with a heavy heart. In his will, written some years later, he praised his 'dearest spouse' of 'blessed memory'. Jane Dawson comments that Marjory's 'faith had quietly helped Knox's own, and she had brought him great personal happiness in their five years of marriage. She had become the perfect minister's wife and gave her husband two sons.'[28] Calvin wrote to Knox, 'Your distress for the loss of your wife commands my deepest sympathy. Persons of her merit are not often to be met with. But as you have well learned from what source consolation for your sorrow is to be sought, I doubt not but you endure with patience this calamity.' Elizabeth Bowes, Knox's mother-in-law, stayed on in Scotland to care for Knox's two sons until he remarried in 1564.

'One Mass is more fearful to me than ten thousand armed enemies.'

In 1561, after the death of her husband Francis II of France, Mary, Queen of Scots came home to Scotland to assume her rule. She had been sent to France at the age of five and had remained there for twelve years. She went to France as a Scot and a Stuart; she returned French and a Guise. Her first Sunday in Scotland, Mary had the Mass said in the Palace of Holyroodhouse. Knox thundered against this act of idolatry from his pulpit in St Giles', and the battle between the Reformer and the queen began. Knox was convinced that Scotland could not have both Reformation and the Roman Catholic Church. He declared that 'one Mass is more fearful to me than if ten thousand armed enemies were landed in any part of the realm to suppress the whole religion'.

'I pray God, Madam, that you may be as blessed within the Commonwealth of Scotland, if it be the pleasure of God, as ever Deborah was in the Commonwealth of Israel.'

On five occasions the queen ordered Knox to appear before her at the palace.[29] In their first meeting, just seven days after Mary arrived from France, she accused Knox of creating rebellion against her mother and herself. Knox stated that he was 'well content' to live under her rule 'as Paul was to live under Nero'! But he insisted that 'subjects are not bound to the religion of their princes, although they are commanded to give them obedience'. He told her that 'God craves of kings that they be foster fathers to his church, and commands queens to be nurses to his people.' In a magnificent conclusion, Knox said, 'I pray God, Madam, that you may be as blessed within the Commonwealth of Scotland, if it be the pleasure of God, as ever Deborah was in the Commonwealth of Israel.' Knox, however, was not hopeful. He found in the queen 'a proud mind, a crafty wit, and an indurate heart against God and his truth'. In a sermon preached some time later, Knox prayed, 'O Lord! For your great name's sake, give to us princes that delight in your truth, that love virtue, hate impiety, and that desire rather to be soundly taught to their salvation than deceivably flattered to their everlasting confusion.'

The second meeting between Mary and Knox took place on December 15, 1562. Knox accused Mary of celebrating the persecutions of the Huguenots in France, and Mary accused Knox of preaching a sermon to 'bring her into hatred and contempt of the people'. He urged her to attend his sermons so that she would hear for herself what he said, or if she preferred he would come to the palace and preach the sermon to her there!

In their third meeting, on April 13 or 14, 1563, Knox and Mary discussed many matters during a long conversation. The queen promised Knox that she would rule with justice.

He replied, 'I am assured then that you shall please God and enjoy rest and tranquillity within your realm; which to Your Majesty is more profitable than all the pope's power can be.'

'Albeit I be neither earl, lord, nor baron in Scotland, yet God has made me a profitable member within the same.'

Knox preached a sermon in St Giles' in which his opponents, and even some of his friends, thought that he had gone too far, when he denounced the queen's proposed marriage to Don Carlos, the son of Philip II of Spain. Knox remembered only too well that Mary Tudor's marriage to the Roman Catholic heir to the Spanish throne had led to the persecution of Protestants in England. Mary, Queen of Scots was infuriated with Knox and called him to the palace to receive her rebuke. He answered: 'Outside the preaching place, Madam, I think few have occasion to be offended at me. There, Madam, I am not master of myself, but must obey him who commands me to speak plain, and to flatter no flesh upon the face of the earth.'

Mary demanded, 'What have you to do with my marriage? Or what are you within this commonwealth?' Knox answered with famous words, 'A subject born within the same, Madam. And albeit I be neither earl, lord, nor baron within it, yet God has made me—however abject I may be in your eyes—a profitable member within the same.'

When Mary burst into angry tears, Knox said, 'Madam, in God's presence I speak. Seeing I have offered to you no just occasion to be offended, but have spoken the truth as my vocation demands, I must sustain, albeit unwillingly, Your Majesty's tears, rather than dare hurt my conscience or betray my commonwealth through my silence.' Knox added, 'I never delighted in the weeping of any of God's creatures. I can scarcely well abide the tears of my own boys whom my own hand corrects; much less can I rejoice in Your Majesty's weeping.'

> *'I am in the place where I am demanded of conscience to speak the truth, and therefore the truth I speak.'*

Because of his outspoken sermons, Knox was tried for treason before the Privy Council in 1563. When he spoke out about 'the insatiable cruelty of the papists within this realm', he was told, 'You forget yourself; you are not now in the pulpit.' Knox replied, 'I am in the place where I am demanded of conscience to speak the truth, and therefore the truth I speak.' Knox reminded the queen that she had insisted that he had nothing to do with her marriage, and that he had replied: 'As touching nature, I was a worm of this earth, and yet a subject of this commonwealth; but as touching the office whereinto it had pleased God to place me, I was a watchman, both over the realm and over the kirk of God gathered within the same; by reason whereof I was bound in conscience to blow the trumpet publicly, so often as I saw any appearing danger, either to the one or to the other.'

One of Knox's critics told him that he would 'find that men will not bear with you in times to come as they have done in times past'. Knox replied: 'If God stand as my friend, as I am assured he of his mercy will, so long as I depend upon his promise, and prefer his glory to my life and worldly profit, I little regard how men behave themselves towards me. Neither do I yet know how any man has borne with me in times past, unless it is because by my mouth they have heard the word of God, which in times to come, if they refuse, my heart will be pierced, and for a season will lament; but the disadvantage will be their own.'

'My Meg.'

In the spring of 1564 Knox married Margaret Stewart, daughter of his great friend Andrew Stewart, Lord Ochiltree. She was seventeen and he was about fifty. 'Large gaps in second marriages were not uncommon during this period,' comments Jane Dawson, 'because older men often sought wives among women of child-bearing age.'[30] Knox came to rely heavily upon his 'Meg'. As well as being the mother of their three daughters, she became his secretary, companion, and nurse.

Knox's second wife was related by blood to Mary, Queen of Scots. The queen was incensed because her royal connections gave Knox a higher social standing within the realm. Marriage to Margaret Stewart also gave Knox another tie to Ayrshire, 'where the radical and uncompromising Protestantism of the faithful brethren flourished', he wrote.

'Be merciful to me, O Lord.'

In his last years Knox was often troubled and even despondent, fearing that the Reformation in Scotland would be compromised or even lost. In a dark hour he wrote that the troubles of a single day were worse than the months of torture he experienced in the galleys. His own failures troubled him. In 1566 he wrote a prayer in which he confessed his sins, praised God for saving and using him, and expressed his longing for death.

'Lord Jesus, receive my spirit, and put an end at your good pleasure to this my miserable life; for justice and truth are not to be found among the sons of men!

'Be merciful to me, O Lord, and call not into judgment my manifold sins; and chiefly those of which the world is not able to accuse me. In youth, middle age, and now, after many battles, I find nothing in me but vanity and corruption. For, in quietness I am negligent, in trouble impatient, tending to desperation; and in the average state, I am so carried away with vain imaginations that, alas, O Lord, they withdraw me from the presence of your majesty. Pride and ambition assault me on the one part, covetousness and malice trouble me on the other: briefly, O Lord, the affections of the flesh almost suppress the operation of your Spirit.

'I take you, O Lord, who alone knows the secrets of hearts, to record that in none of the aforesaid do I delight, but that with them I am troubled, and that painfully against the desire of my inward man, which sobs for my corruption and would repose in your mercy alone. I claim the promise that you have made to all penitent sinners, of whose number I profess myself to be one, in the obedience and death of my only Saviour, our Lord Jesus Christ. In whom, by your mere grace, I doubt not myself to be elected to eternal salvation, of which you have given to me—to me, O Lord, most wretched and unthankful creature—most assured signs.

'For being drowned in my ignorance, you have given to me knowledge above the common sort of my brethren; my tongue you have used to set forth your glory, to fight against idolatry, errors, and false doctrine. You have compelled me to speak forth deliverance to the afflicted and destruction to certain disobedient; the performance whereof, not I alone but the very blind world has already seen. But above all, O Lord, you, by the power of your Holy Spirit, have sealed into my heart remission of my sins, which I acknowledge and confess myself to have received by the precious blood of Jesus Christ once shed; by whose perfect obedience I am assured my manifold rebellions are defaced, my grievous sins purged, and my soul made the tabernacle of your godly majesty. You, O Father of mercies, your Son our Lord Jesus, my only Saviour, Mediator, and Advocate, and your Holy Spirit, remaining in the same true faith; which is the only victory that overcomes the world.

'To you, therefore, O Lord, I commend my spirit; for I thirst to be resolved from this body of sin, and am assured that I shall rise again in glory, howsoever it may be that the wicked, for a time, shall tread me and others of your servants under their feet. Be merciful, O Lord, to the kirk within this realm; continue with it the light of your evangel; augment the number of true preachers; and let your merciful providence look upon my desolate bedfellow, our three children, and my two other dear children, Nathaniel and Eleazar. Now Lord, put end to my misery!'

'God, who from my youth has provided, will,
of his mercy, still minister such things as
he knows expedient for me.'

Knox was busy writing his *History of the Reformation in Scotland*. He began the preface to Book IV with words of encouragement, reminding himself and the faithful that their strength came from the Lord: 'In the former books, gentle reader, you may clearly see how potently God has performed, in these our last and wicked days as well as in ages before us, the promises made to the servants of God by the prophet Isaiah, "They that wait upon the Lord shall renew their strength; they shall lift up the wings as the eagles: they shall run and not be weary; they shall walk, and not faint.'"

In a letter to Christopher Goodman, Knox wrote that he would be glad to see his friend again 'if it was but one day before God should put an end to my troubles, which time I am assured approaches very near. The state of things with us I cannot nor will not write, for grief and shame do both forbid.' On a lighter note, Knox wrote that 'my Meg commends you to God', and added humorously that she was so taken up with their baby daughter Martha 'that all service is gone'.

Knox left Edinburgh in March 1566 and was happily living and preaching among his wife's relatives in Ayrshire. The ageing Knox was 'troubled having little here to furnish a house', but was encouraged when he remembered that 'God, who from my youth has provided, will, of his mercy, still minister such things as he knows expedient for me'. Many in Edinburgh wanted their former minister back, but he was not eager to return to the city, obtaining instead a roving preaching commission from the General Assembly.

In 1567 Knox made a trip to England to visit Elizabeth Bowes, his mother-in-law, and his two sons.[31] Knox happily met some people who had been members of the English church in Geneva when he was their pastor. He wrote:

'God comfort that dispersed little flock, among whom I once lived with quietness of conscience and contentment of heart; and among whom I would be content to end my days, if so it might stand with God's good pleasure.' Thinking of the continuing turmoil in Scotland, Knox said, 'I cannot but love the quietness of England because in that realm God has many faithful hearts although they be few if they be compared with the multitude of the wicked.'

'The only deliverance is to know God.'

Knox wrote to Christopher Goodman, who was then serving as a preacher in Ireland, 'God make your labours no less fruitful than were the labours of Titus in the island of Crete.' Knox seriously considered Goodman's proposal that he join him in Ireland, but felt that without the permission of the General Assembly he could not leave his church in Ayr nor his congregation at St Giles' in Edinburgh, which still had a claim on him. He wrote to Goodman that he could not come to Ireland because 'I dare not cast off that burden that God has laid upon me to preach to unthankful (yea, alas, miserable) Scotland.'

In another letter to Goodman, Knox began with a prayer in Latin. In English translation it reads: 'Lord Jesus, arise and defend your people; do not allow Satan to pour forth his empty opinion in place of true faith, to advance the dead letter in place of the living word of God, to induce doubt in place of certainty and darkness in place of light.'

After thanking God for Goodman and his friendship, Knox quoted 2 Timothy 4:1-2, followed by these lines: 'And now to say a little of myself that I am of this mind. If you learn to know Christ, it is enough, even if you are ignorant of other things. If you learn to know other things, it is nothing, if you are ignorant of Christ. The only deliverance is to know God; other things are deceptions.'

Eventually Knox returned to Edinburgh. He wrote to Goodman, 'I have given myself to serve his poor flock in this town so long as ten of them will remain together and crave to hear.' Knox stayed in the city during a severe plague, even though both Roman Catholic and Protestant 'principal men' left for safer places.[32]

Facing the hostility of the supporters of the queen, including some who had been his friends, Knox was depressed. Thinking that his death was not far away, he sent a farewell letter to Goodman: 'Now, brother, if it please my God to call me from this misery before I shall have the occasion to write to you again, rejoice with me that it has pleased the mercy of our God to make us agree so long in the midst of divers temptations in the simplicity of his truth. Your friendship has been comfortable to me in many ways, especially for the uprightness of judgment, which I never saw corrupted in you for any worldly cause, in which integrity I pray God, for Christ Jesus his Son's sake, you may continue to the end. Amen.'

'Pray for me, brethren, that I may fight my battle lawfully to the end.'

Against the background of the religious and political struggle, Queen Mary's personal life played itself out in unfortunate marriages, scenes of violence and murder, and, finally, flight from Scotland, leaving her infant son, James VI, as a 'cradle' king. Knox never forgave Mary, Queen of Scots, and warned others not to give in to 'foolish pity' for her. Many, including Knox, thought that Mary deserved the death penalty for adultery and murder. She was eventually executed, not by Scottish Presbyterians but by her English cousin, Queen Elizabeth, 'so ending one of the saddest dramas of all history'.[33]

Knox gladly gave his attention to his primary calling, the preaching of the gospel, but he could not resist making strong and pointed applications in his sermons to matters of government. His enemies, and even some of his friends, wanted the controversial preacher out of Edinburgh. Knox had strong support from Protestants in Ayrshire, 'the brethren of the West', who wrote to defend him whose life was as dear to them, they said, as their own. 'God has made him both the first planter, and also the chief waterer of his kirk among us. In his protection and life (to our judgment) stands the prosperity and increase of God's kirk and religion.'

Knox left Edinburgh, and on May 7, 1571 arrived in St Andrews, 'sore against his will', he said. Knox preached weekly and when he was able visited St Leonard's College where he would sit in a chair in the yard, talking with and blessing the students, exhorting them 'to know God and his work on our country, and stand by the good cause'.

James Melville, a student at St Andrews at the time, wrote in his diary: 'Of all the benefits I had that year was the coming of that most notable prophet and apostle of our nation, Mr John Knox, to St Andrews. I heard him teach the prophecy of Daniel that summer. I had my pen and my little book, and took away such things as I could comprehend. In the opening up of his text he was moderate for the space of an half-hour; but when he entered to application, he made me so to shudder and tremble that I could not hold a pen to write.'[34]

Knox wrote to the congregation in Edinburgh: 'Be faithful and loving one to another. Let bitterness and suspicion be far out of your hearts. Rejoice in the Lord that he has counted you worthy to suffer for his name's sake. Pray for me, brethren, that I may fight my battle lawfully to the end. The Lord Jesus preserve you now and ever! Amen.'

'God was pleased of his grace to make me a steward of divine mysteries.'

The St Giles' congregation—'your brethren and children in God'—sent a letter to Knox, urging him to come to them so that 'once again your voice might be heard among us'. Knox, with his wife and three daughters, returned to

Edinburgh, where they lived in a house near St Giles', now known as the 'John Knox House'.[35] Knox preached there until his last sermon on November 9, 1572. Thomas Smeton, later principal of the University of Glasgow, described the scene: 'After he had pronounced a blessing upon the people, with a mind more cheerful than usual but with a weak body and leaning upon his staff, he departed, accompanied by almost the whole assembly, to his house, from which he did not again come forth in life.'

On November 17, Knox called the elders and deacons to his bedside to say his goodbyes and to 'exhort them to stand constant in that doctrine which they had heard of his mouth, however unworthy that he was'. Others came too, so that the scene in the house half-way along the Royal Mile was like that at the end of the *Pilgrim's Progress*, 'where a great concourse of pilgrims accompany Mr Valiant-for-Truth to the riverside'.[36] Knox said: 'I know that many have complained much and loudly, and do still complain of my too-great severity; but God knows that my mind was always free from hatred to the persons of those against whom I denounced the heavy judgments of God. In the meantime, I cannot deny but that I felt the greatest abhorrence of the sin in which they indulged; still, however, keeping this one thing in view, that if it were possible I might gain them to the Lord. But a certain reverential fear of my God who called me, and was pleased of his grace to make me a steward of divine mysteries, to whom I knew I must render an account, when I shall appear before his tribunal, of the manner in which I have discharged the embassy which he has committed to me—had such a powerful effect as to make me utter intrepidly whatever the Lord put into my mouth, without respect of persons. Therefore, I profess before God and his holy angels that I never made gain of the sacred word of God, that I never studied to please men, never indulged my own private passions or those of others, but faithfully distributed the talent entrusted to my care for the edification of the church over which I did watch.'

'I see permanent joy to come after trouble.'

On one occasion Knox preached a sermon on a favourite text, Isaiah 26:19: 'Your dead shall live; their bodies shall rise. You who dwell in the dust, awake and sing for joy! For your dew is a dew of light, and the earth will give birth to the dead.' In it the preacher uttered words that beautifully summed up his testimony and sustained him in his last days.

'The prophet here pierces through all impediments that nature could object; and by the victory of faith, he overcomes not only the common enemies but the great and last enemy of all, death itself. For this would he say: Lord, I see nothing to your chosen but misery to follow misery, and one affliction to succeed another; yea, in the end I see that death shall devour your dearest children. But yet, O Lord, I see your promise to be true, and your love to remain toward your chosen, even when death appears to have devoured them: "For your dead shall live, yea, not only shall they live, but my very dead body shall arise." And so I see honour and glory to succeed this temporal shame; I see permanent joy to come after trouble, order to spring out of this terrible confusion; and, finally, I see that life shall devour death, so that death shall be destroyed, and so your servants shall have life.'

'I have been in meditation these last two nights concerning the troubled church of God.'

November 24, 1572 was John Knox's last day on earth. He said, 'I have been in meditation these last two nights concerning the troubled church of God, the spouse of Jesus Christ, despised of the world but precious in his sight. I have called to God for her, and have committed her to her head, Jesus Christ.' A little after noon, he asked his wife to read the fifteenth chapter of 1 Corinthians. Some hours later he said to her, 'Go, read where I cast my first anchor', and she read the seventeenth chapter of John's Gospel. Family and friends gathered around his bed for evening prayers. When someone asked if he had heard the psalm-singing and prayers, Knox replied, 'I would to God that you and all men heard them as I have heard them; and I praise God for that heavenly sound.' A little later Knox gave a long sigh and said, 'Now it is done.' When asked by a friend to give a sign that he remembered Christ's promises, Knox raised his hand and slipped away without any pain.

From John Knox's house the funeral procession moved to St Giles' churchyard on November 26. Robert Louis Stevenson wrote that 'the ancient burying ground of Edinburgh behind St Giles' Church has disappeared, and for those ignorant of its history, I know only one token that remains. Two letters and a date mark the resting place of the man who made Scotland over again in his own image, the indefatigable, undissuadable John Knox. He sleeps within call of the church that so often echoed to his preaching.'[37]

Endnotes

[1] *The Works of John Knox*, edited by David Lang (Edinburgh, 1895; repr. Edinburgh: Banner of Truth Trust, 2014), contains almost all that Knox wrote. A convenient edition of Knox's *History of the Reformation of Religion within the Realm of Scotland*, edited for popular use by C. J. Guthrie, was reprinted by the Banner of Truth Trust in 1982. *Selected Writings of John Knox: Public Epistles, Treatises, and Expositions to the Year 1559* was published in 1995 by Presbyterian Heritage Publications. The text is edited to reflect contemporary spelling, punctuation, and grammar. *The Select Practical Writings of John Knox* (first published in 1845 by the Free Church of Scotland) was reprinted in a new edition by the Banner of Truth Trust, Edinburgh, 2011. Two useful biographies of Knox are *Trumpeter of God* by W. Stanford Reid (New York: Charles Scribner's Sons, 1974) and *John Knox* by Jane Dawson (New Haven: Yale University Press, 2015). Reid describes Knox 'as a man who sought to accomplish a certain purpose, and who attained considerable success, yet who at the same time had

all the weaknesses, failings and foibles of every man, but who has had an influence on history down to the present day' (286). Dawson hopes that her book 'will offer the reader the opportunity to follow John Knox through his life, to see his many public and private faces and perhaps encounter a few surprises' (10). Reid's book is sympathetic, though not uncritical. Dawson's work is thorough and scholarly but at times judges Knox more harshly than necessary.

[2] Henry R. Sefton, *John Knox: An Account of the Development of His Spirituality* (Edinburgh: Saint Andrew Press, 1993), 33. Sefton's little book, part of *The Devotional Library of Saint Andrew Press*, aims 'to let John Knox speak, as far as possible, for himself and to show how the circumstances of his life shaped the style of his spirituality' (ix).

[3] Reid, *Trumpeter of God*, 203.

[4] R. M. Healey, 'John Knox's "History": A "Compleat" Sermon on Christian Duty', *Church History* 61 (1992), 333.

[5] Dawson, *John Knox*, 266.

[6] David Murison, 'Knox the Writer', in *John Knox: A Quartercentenary Reappraisal* (Edinburgh: St Andrew Press, 1975), 46.

[7] In 1881, at the site of the house where Knox was thought to have been born, an oak tree was planted 'after the wish of the late Thomas Carlyle', according to the inscription on a nearby stone.

[8] Hamilton's initials mark the place of his martyrdom outside St Salvator's Chapel in North Street, St Andrews.

[9] Reid, *Trumpeter of God*, 25.

[10] Wishart refers to the young boys Knox was teaching.

[11] 'The gentlest and most reverent pages in all Knox's *History* are those in which he tells of the courage of George Wishart at his trial and his constancy in the hour of death' (*The History of the Reformation*, 65, f. 1).

[12] Reid, *Trumpeter of God*, 36. Reid writes that the motivation of this group was 'very mixed, with the predominant element purely secular'.

[13] Geddes MacGregor, *The Thundering Scot: A Portrait of John Knox* (Philadelphia: Westminster Press, 1957), 46. In an essay 'The Galleys of France', W. H. Lewis (historian and brother of C. S. Lewis) wrote: 'Until the coming of the concentration camp, the galley held an undisputed pre-eminence as the darkest blot on Western civilization; a galley, said a poetic observer shudderingly, would cast a shadow in the blackest midnight.' *Essays Presented to Charles Williams*, edited by C. S. Lewis (Grand Rapids: William B. Eerdmans Publishing Company, 1966), 136.

[14] Reid, *Trumpeter of God*, 57.

[15] Reid, *Trumpeter of God*, 80.

[16] Often spelled 'Locke', as in John Locke who descended from the same family.

[17] Susan M. Felch, '"Deir Sister": The Letters of John Knox to Anne Vaughan Lok', *Renaissance and Reformation* 19 (1995), 62.

[18] *The Catholic Encyclopedia,* Charles George Herbermann, ed., with others (Knights of Columbus, 1907–1912) 8:684.

[19] See Jane Dawson and Lionel K. J. Glassey, 'Some Unpublished Letters from John Knox to Christopher Goodman', *The Scottish Historical Review* 84 (2005), 166-201.

[20] Sir David Wilkie (1785–1841), the most celebrated Scottish artist of the early nineteenth century, produced an unfinished painting, 'John Knox Administering the Sacrament of the Lord's Supper at Calder House'.

[21] Dawson, *John Knox*, 1.

[22] R. Ward Holder, 'John Knox Revisited', in *Expository Times*, August 2015, 526.

[23] C. S. Lewis, *English Literature in the Sixteenth Century* (New York: Oxford University Press, 1954), 200.

[24] *History of the Reformation in Scotland*, 171, f. 1. Thomas Carlyle wrote, 'Knox wanted no pulling down of stone edifices; he wanted leprosy and darkness to be thrown out of the lives of men. Tumult was not his element; it was the tragic feature of his life that he was forced to dwell so much in that' (180, f. 1).

[25] Reid, *Trumpeter of God*, 173. David Wilkie's painting of 'John Knox preaching at St Andrews' on June 11, 1559 dramatically depicts this scene.

[26] Reid, *Trumpeter of God*, 186-87.

[27] David Wright, 'John Knox's Bible', in *The Bible As Book: The Reformation*, ed. Orlath O'Sullivan (London: The British Library & Oak Knoll Press, 2000), 59.

[28] Dawson, *John Knox*, 205.

[29] Some have accused Knox of angry outbursts against the queen in these discussions, but he does not appear to have been overbearing or disrespectful. Thomas Carlyle writes that Knox's speeches to Mary 'seem to me about as fine as the circumstances would permit'.

[30] Dawson, *John Knox*, 229.

[31] Both his sons went up to St John's College, Cambridge, eventually serving as ministers of the Church of England.

[32] Dawson and Glassey, 'Some Unpublished Letters from John Knox to Christopher Goodman', 195.

[33] MacGregor, *The Thundering Scot*, 215.

[34] James Melville, *The Autobiography and Diary of James Melvill* [sic] (Edinburgh, 1842).

[35] The John Knox House was built sometime before 1490, and is said to be the oldest house in Edinburgh. It was probably the residence of the Reformer during a portion of the last years of his life.

[36] Charles John Guthrie, *John Knox and John Knox's House* (Edinburgh: Oliphant Anderson and Ferrier, 1905), 80.

[37] Robert Louis Stevenson, *Edinburgh: Picturesque Notes* (London: Pallas Athene, 2001), 34-35. The graveyard has been paved over, but Knox's burial spot is located by a plaque in a parking space (#23). The old plaque which read 'I K 1572' (representing Iohannes Knox) has been replaced with one that reads: 'The above stone marks the approximate site of the burial place in St Giles' Graveyard of John Knox the great Scottish divine who died 24 Nov. 1572.'

4

John Bunyan's Testimony

The sixty years of John Bunyan's life were 'the most turbulent, seditious, and factious sixty years of recorded English history'.[1] When Bunyan was born in 1628, Charles I was king, having succeeded his father, James I (James VI of Scotland), in 1625. Bunyan lived through the Civil War and the execution of King Charles, the Commonwealth of Oliver Cromwell, and the Restoration of the monarchy in 1660. He died in 1688, just before the abdication of James II and the coronation of William and Mary, and the Toleration Act of 1689.

The main source for the life of John Bunyan is his autobiography, *Grace Abounding to the Chief of Sinners*, first published in 1666. Marcus Loane writes that *Grace Abounding* 'will always retain its place as one of the finest records of a profound spiritual experience'.[2] It is Bunyan's testimony, the story of how God saved him. It is also a sermon. Rebecca Beal calls it 'John Bunyan's Pauline Epistle'. Its title reflects 'a major emphasis of Pauline epistles: salvation by grace alone'.[3] Alexander Whyte writes that 'the very title of this spiritual masterpiece ... may very well be taken as the title of every genuine Puritan sermon; that is to say: first, sin abounding, and then grace much more abounding'.[4]

Bunyan tells his story with simplicity and seriousness. He wrote: 'God did not play in convincing of me, the devil did not play in tempting of me, neither did I play when I sunk as into a bottomless pit, when the pangs of hell caught hold upon me; wherefore I may not play in my relating of them, but be plain and simple, and lay down the thing as it was.' Bunyan leaves out many of the facts of his life, but sets forth in excruciating detail the spiritual agony and uncertainty that tormented him until he was finally brought to spiritual peace and assurance of his salvation. He aptly describes his book as 'something of a relation of the work of God upon my own soul, even from the very first until now, in which you may perceive my castings down, and raisings up; for he wounds, and his hands make whole'.

It was a requirement in the Bedford congregation which Bunyan joined in 1655 (as well as in other Puritan churches) that new members make a public testimony of their conversion before being admitted as full members. *Grace Abounding* is a greatly expanded version of Bunyan's testimony to his church. He had been in prison for five or six years before he wrote the book to 'further edify and build up in faith and holiness' his fellow Christians.

Bunyan expanded *Grace Abounding* through six editions, giving further information about earlier events and adding material based on later happenings. Sections 306–17 were added to the fifth edition as an answer to slanderous charges that had been made about Bunyan. Several additional sections, or pastoral letters, complete the book: 'A Brief Account of the Author's Call to the Work of the Ministry', followed by 'A Relation of My Imprisonment'. The latter is a series of practically verbatim reports of Bunyan's examination before the justices.

These may have been written in prison immediately after the events, as pastoral letters to console and fortify the Bedford congregation. There are five short narratives, each ending with an epistolary formula such as 'Farewell'.

'My father's house was of that rank that is meanest and most despised of all the families in the land.'

John Bunyan was born in the small village of Elstow, just south of Bedford on the road to London, in south-central England. He says little about his family and early years, giving only a 'hint of his pedigree that thereby the goodness and bounty of God towards him may be magnified'. Bunyan was born 'of a low and inconsiderable generation', he wrote, 'my father's house being of that rank that is meanest and most despised of all the families in the land'. His father, 'a repairer of pans and kettles', pushed a small wooden cart around the countryside, sometimes carrying his sixty-pound anvil on his back.

John was the oldest child of his father's second marriage. His childhood, he wrote, was filled with 'fearful dreams' and 'thoughts of the day of judgment'. He was twice saved from drowning while swimming in the river and once survived a violent fever. Bunyan later wrote that 'the elect are saved before they are called', that is, their lives are spared until effectual saving grace reaches their souls.

John's mother died when he was sixteen, and a sad few weeks later his sister Margaret died. The next month his father remarried. His father was not a godly man, and from him his son learned to speak, as he did, with 'this wicked way of swearing'. Nonetheless John seems to have loved his father and hoped for his conversion. In his catechism for children Bunyan wrote that children should pray for their parents that 'the Lord, if it be his will, convert our poor parents, that they, with us, may be the children of God'. When his father died in 1676, Bunyan described in a passage in the book he was writing at the time how the ministering spirits or angels of Hebrews 1:14 take charge of the soul of the dying Christian. 'Neither our meanness in the world, nor our weakness of faith' will hinder God's angels in conducting us 'safely to glory', he wrote.

'When I was a soldier ...'

The Civil War erupted in England during the summer of 1642. The king and the parliament were on a collision course, and both raised armies. Sixteen-year-old Bunyan enlisted to serve with the Parliamentary army. He was stationed at Newport Pagnell, some fifteen miles from home. He probably saw little military action, but he experienced the rough life of a soldier and came into contact with the religious and political ferment of the time. In *Grace Abounding* he makes just one brief reference to the time of his military service. 'When I was a soldier, I, with others, was drawn out to go to such a place to besiege it; but when I was just ready to go, one of the company desired to go in my place; to which, when I had consented, he took my place; and coming to the siege, as he stood sentinel, he was shot in the head with a musket bullet and died.' Bunyan experienced both 'judgments and mercy, but neither of them did awaken my soul to righteousness', he confessed. In one of his later books Bunyan stated that he was persuaded that 'did men believe that there is that grace and willingness in the heart of Christ to save sinners, as the word imports there is, they would come tumbling into his arms'. But it would be some time before Bunyan would come tumbling to Christ.

The Parliamentary victory at Naseby in June 1645 essentially ended the war. Parliament brought Charles I to public trial and execution, abolished the House of Lords, and proclaimed England a Commonwealth with Oliver Cromwell ruling as 'Lord Protector'.

'I grew more and more rebellious against God.'

Bunyan went home to Elstow, where he became the ringleader of a group of idle young men given to swearing and breaking the strict Puritan Sabbath. In one of his last writings, *Good News for the Vilest of Men*, Bunyan remembered how he 'infected the youth of the town with all manner of youthful vanities'. 'Sin and corruption would as naturally bubble out of my heart as water would bubble out of a fountain. I grew more and more rebellious against God, and careless of my own salvation,' he wrote.

> *The books 'did not reach my heart, to awaken it about my sad and sinful state, yet they did beget within me some desires to religion'.*

Sometime in 1649 the twenty-one-year-old Bunyan married. We know almost nothing about his wife, not even her name. Henri Talon writes that she 'was a model woman, and the faith from which she drew her inspiration made a direct call to Bunyan's soul. She brought him a tender love, but it only awakened his thirst for higher joys.'[5] Their first child, a daughter born blind and named Mary, was baptized on July 20, 1650.

The young Bunyans were so poor that they did not have, he wrote, 'so much household stuff as a dish or a spoon between us both'. They did have two books, inherited from Bunyan's father-in-law—Lewis Bayly's *Practice of Piety* and Arthur Dent's *Plain Man's Pathway to Heaven*. John and his wife read the books together. 'Though they did not reach my heart to awaken it,' he wrote, 'yet they did beget within me some desires to religion.'

What followed for Bunyan was an intense and prolonged period of spiritual crises, in which his agony of doubt and confusion occasionally gave way to brief times of hope, but these did not last. Like his pilgrim in *Pilgrim's Progress*, with a burden on his back and a Bible in his hand, Bunyan made a slow and painful journey from unbelief to faith and finally to assurance. Bunyan knew that his struggle was especially severe. He said in a sermon later in life, 'Perhaps God will deal more gently with you than with me; if so thank him for it.'

'My neighbours were amazed at my great conversion from prodigious profaneness to something like a moral life.'

John Bunyan fell in 'very eagerly with the religion of the times', going to church faithfully. He became devoted to 'the high place, priest, clerk, vestment, service' and everything else belonging to the Church of England. 'My neighbours were amazed at this my great conversion, from prodigious profaneness to something like a moral life,' Bunyan wrote. 'But all this while, I was not sensible of the danger and evil of sin; I was kept from considering that sin would damn me, whatever religion I followed, unless I was found in Christ.'

Despite his outward reformation, Bunyan was troubled by what he thought were damning sins. He was addicted to Sunday sports. One Sunday he was convicted by a sermon from the parson, but he succeeded, he said, in shaking the sermon out of his mind and went on with his games. In the middle of a game of 'tipcat',[6] just as he was ready to strike a second blow, 'a voice did suddenly dart from heaven into my soul, which said, "Will you leave your sins and go to heaven, or have your sins and go to hell?"' Bunyan felt that he was too great a sinner to be forgiven, and so decided to go on in his sin. In fact, he feared that he would die before he could enjoy to the full his sinful life.

Bunyan also worried about his love of bell-ringing. He became fearful that the great bells would fall on him, or even that the steeple of the church would collapse and kill him. Finally, with much difficulty, he gave up bell-ringing and Sunday sports. It was even harder for him to renounce dancing. As Talon wisely explains, 'Only Bunyan knew why he had to stop dancing, playing bowls and ringing bells. But to anyone who knows anything about [Puritan souls], their petty renunciations, far from raising a smile, will seem like so many acts of heroism.'[7] It is interesting and significant that games, bell-ringing, and dancing were surrendered by Bunyan the sinner and celebrated by Bunyan the saint in his many writings.

Despite his efforts to reform, Bunyan 'went on in sin with great greediness of mind'. When he was rebuked by an ungodly woman for his cursing and swearing, it silenced and shamed him. He wished with all his heart that he might be a little child again so that he could learn to speak 'without this wicked way of swearing'.

Bunyan now believed that 'it was now too late' for him to hope for heaven, but God was not finished with him. A passage in one of his books, *Christ a Complete Saviour*, reads: 'Consider, also, that he has made a beginning with your soul to reconcile you to God, and to that end has bestowed his justice upon you, put his Spirit within you, and has begun to make the unweldable mountain and rock, your heart, to turn towards him, and desire after him; to believe in him, and rejoice in him.'

'I set the Ten Commandments before me for my way to heaven.'

'I set the Commandments before me for my way to heaven,' Bunyan said. Not only were his neighbours impressed; so was he. 'I thought I pleased God as well as any man in England,' he wrote. But Bunyan knew that he was 'a poor painted hypocrite', yet he 'loved to be talked of as one that was truly godly'. He was 'a brisk talker in the matters of religion', he said, not unlike his character 'Talkative' in *Pilgrim's Progress*.

In *Saved by Grace* Bunyan wrote that he made vows to God and broke them, repenting and promising to do better next time. He was 'feeding God with chapters, and prayers, and promises, and vows, and a great many more such dainty dishes, and thinking that he serves God as well as any man in England can, while he has only got into a cleaner way to hell than the rest of his neighbours are in'. He was still ignorant of the fact that salvation was not achieved by his own righteousness but by the mercy of God in Christ. He did not yet know, he wrote, 'Christ, nor grace, nor faith, nor hope'.

One day I met 'three or four poor but pious happy women sitting at a door in the sun and talking about the things of God.'

One day, as John worked as a tinker in Bedford, he came upon 'three or four poor but pious happy women sitting at a door in the sun and talking about the things of God', as they twisted bobbins to make lace. He came closer to hear what they were saying and quickly realized that 'they were far above' him in spiritual matters, 'for their talk was about a new birth, the work of God on their hearts. They talked of how God had visited their souls with his love in the Lord Jesus, and with what words and promises they had been refreshed, comforted, and supported against the temptations of the devil.' 'They spoke,' Bunyan wrote, 'as if joy did make them speak.' He was greatly affected by their words, words that went far deeper than Bunyan's external religious observances. They 'enshrined key Reformation principles' such as justification by faith, writes Michael Mullett.[8]

The meeting with the women caused Bunyan's thoughts to be 'fixed on eternity'. He began to read the Bible 'with new eyes, especially the epistles of the apostle Paul were sweet and pleasant to me'. Earlier he had read 'the historical part' of the Bible, but could not understand Paul's epistles, and Scriptures of that nature, 'being as yet but ignorant either of the corruptions of my nature or of the want and worth of Jesus Christ to save me'. Now, as he put it, 'I was never out of the Bible, either by reading or meditation; still crying out to God that I might know the truth, and the way to heaven and glory.'

I dreamed that I found 'a narrow gap, like a little doorway in the wall'.

Before long, however, Bunyan was again assailed by fears and doubts. He was troubled especially by two questions—'Do I have faith?' and 'Am I one of the elect?' Hours of joy and days of torment followed each other closely. One day the idea came to him that if he were of the elect he should be able to work miracles. As he walked on the road, he was tempted to try to make the puddles dry up and the dry places fill with water.

Then in 'a dream or vision' Bunyan saw 'the state and happiness' of the poor people at Bedford. He saw them 'on the sunny side of some high mountain, there refreshing themselves with the pleasant beams of the sun', while he was 'shivering and shrinking in the cold, afflicted with frost, snow, and dark clouds'. Bunyan dreamed that he saw a wall around the mountain with 'a narrow gap, like a little doorway in the wall', that separated him from the sunny side of the mountain. But 'the passage' was 'very strait and narrow' and he could not get through. He struggled until at last he succeeded and 'went and sat down' among the poor people, and was 'comforted with the light and heat of their sun'. Bunyan explained that the mountain was 'the church of the living God', the sun was 'the shining of his merciful face', the wall was 'the word, that did make separation between the Christians and the world', and the gap in the wall was 'Jesus Christ who is the way to God the Father'. 'None could enter into life, but those that were in downright earnest, and unless also they left this wicked world behind them; for here was only room for body and soul, but not for body and soul and sin.'

'And yet there is room.'

Still Bunyan had no assurance that he was 'one of that number that did sit in the sunshine'. Scriptures came to his mind, sometimes to comfort, but often to perplex and condemn him, until he was ready to sink 'with faintness in his mind'. Once he was so troubled that he hardly knew what to do, when the voice of Christ broke in upon his soul, saying, 'Compel them to come in that my house may be filled', and 'yet there is room'. These were 'sweet words to me,' Bunyan wrote, 'for truly I thought that by them I saw there was place enough in heaven for me; and, moreover, that when the Lord Jesus did speak these words, he then did think of me.'

'Holy Mr Gifford, whose doctrine, by God's grace, was much for my stability.'

But the joy did not last, and Bunyan found himself overcome, thinking of his sins, and tempted to 'go back again'.

It appeared that he was making no progress. 'However, the wave that comes in is less strong than the one that goes out,' writes Henri Talon. 'Though buffeted and sometimes submerged, he did make progress.'[9] Through 'those poor people in Bedford', Bunyan met their pastor, John Gifford. Gifford 'was willing to be "well" persuaded of me', Bunyan wrote, 'though I think but from little grounds: but he invited me to his house, where I should hear him confer with others about the dealings of God with the soul; from all of which I still received more conviction, and from that time began to see something of the vanity and inward wretchedness of my wicked heart'.

Bunyan spoke of 'holy Mr Gifford, whose doctrine, by God's grace, was much for my stability'. In *Pilgrim's Progress*, Bunyan paid loving tribute to Gifford. The Bedford pastor appears as Evangelist: 'I saw also that the pilgrim looked this way, and that way, as if he would run; yet he stood still because, as I perceived, he could not tell which way to go. I looked then and saw a man named Evangelist coming to him, and asked Why stand still? He answered, Because I don't know which way to go. Then said Evangelist, pointing with his finger over a very wide field, Do you see yonder wicket-gate? The man said, No. Do you see yonder shining light? He said, I think I do. Then said Evangelist, Keep that light in your eye, and go up directly to it, so you shall see the gate, at which when you knock, it shall be told you what you shall do.'

John Gifford may also be 'the very grave person' whose picture was hanging in Interpreter's House: 'He had eyes lifted up to heaven, the best of books in his hand, the law of truth was written upon his lips, the world was behind his back. He stood as if he pleaded with men, and a crown of gold did hang over his head.' In *Makers of Puritan History*, Marcus Loane writes, 'Bunyan may have had John Gifford in view when he drew this picture, but it is clear that it is an unconscious self-portrait.'[10]

'I am Magdalene, I am Zaccheus, I am the thief, I am the harlot, I am the publican, I am the prodigal.'

Bunyan now more clearly understood the way of salvation. He wrote, 'I saw that I wanted a perfect righteousness to present me without fault before God, and this righteousness was nowhere to be found but in the person of Jesus Christ.' He continued to be troubled, however, that he did not have that righteousness of Christ and never would. His heart was still 'full of longing after God', but he felt trapped by 'wicked thoughts and desires', like a 'clog on the leg of a bird to hinder her from flying'. 'In this condition I went a great while,' he wrote, until he heard a sermon on Song of Solomon 4:1—'Behold, you are fair, my love, behold, you are fair.' This moved him deeply. As he repeated the words 'you are my love' over and over, he found himself 'between hope and fear'. 'Now was my heart filled full of comfort and hope, and now I could believe that my sins should be forgiven me; yea I was now so taken with the love and mercy of God that I remember I could not tell how to contain till I got home; I thought I could have spoken of his love and of his mercy to me even to the very crows that sat upon the ploughed lands before me.'

In one of his last writings Bunyan described the sinner's experience in words of his own testimony.

'It is enough to make angels blush, says Satan, to see so vile a one knock at heaven's gates for mercy, and will you be so abominably bold as to do it?

'Thus Satan dealt with me, says the great sinner, when at first I came to Jesus Christ. And what did you reply? says the tempter. Why, I granted the whole charge to be true, says the other. And what, did you despair, or how? No, says he, I said, I am Magdalene, I am Zaccheus, I am the thief, I am the harlot, I am the publican, I am the prodigal, and one of Christ's murderers; yea, worse than any of these.'

'God did cast into my hand a book of Martin Luther.'

Bunyan's relief was followed by another period of doubt and depression. He began to experience, to his 'great confusion and astonishment', doubts even about the existence of God and Christ and the truthfulness of the Bible. Much to his alarm, he was tempted 'to curse and swear, or to speak some grievous thing against God or Christ, his Son, and of the Scriptures'. He thought that he was 'possessed of the devil'. For about a year he remained in great despair, until

'God in whose hands are all our days and ways did cast into my hand', Bunyan wrote, Martin Luther's *Commentary on Galatians*. 'When I had but a little way perused the book, I found my condition so largely and profoundly handled, as if his book had been written out of my heart.' It was a book, Bunyan wrote, above all books he had ever seen, as 'most fit for a wounded conscience'.

Luther insisted that a person is not justified by the works of the law but by faith in Jesus Christ, as set forth in the words of Paul, 'the just shall live by faith'. The doctrine of justification by faith alone brought great comfort to Martin Luther, who, like John Bunyan after him, had vainly attempted to satisfy God by his own accomplishments, that is, by 'the works of the law'. To Bunyan came a sense of 'those heights and depths in grace and love and mercy', and the assurance that 'great sins do draw out great grace'.

'Return to me, for I have redeemed you.'

Bunyan's spiritual struggle, however, was far from over. Soon Satan tempted him to 'sell and part with this most blessed Christ—to exchange him for the things of this life'. Sometimes the words 'sell him, sell him, sell him' would churn in Bunyan's mind more than a hundred times until he was physically exhausted. Finally, he gave way and thought, 'Let him go, if he will.' 'And down I fell,' Bunyan wrote, 'as a bird that is shot from the top of a tree, into great guilt, and fearful despair.' He was seized with the thought that he was 'bound over to eternal punishment'. The example of Esau, 'who, for one morsel of meat, sold his birthright', plagued him. 'Esau' became a troubling code word for Bunyan, and he returned again and again to the words of Hebrews 12:17—'For you know, how that afterward, when [Esau] would have inherited the blessing, he was rejected; for he found no place of repentance, though he sought it carefully with tears.' These words, Bunyan wrote, 'were to my soul like fetters of brass to my legs'.

But there were moments of relief. 'About ten or eleven o'clock one day, as I was walking under a hedge, full of sorrow and guilt, suddenly this sentence bolted upon me, "The blood of Jesus Christ cleanses us from all sin."' On another day, he heard the text crying out, 'with a very great voice, "Return unto me, for I have redeemed you."' These words, wrote Bunyan, made him stop and, 'as it were, look over my shoulder to see if I could discern that the God of grace did follow me with a pardon in his hand'. But soon he found himself again fearful that he was rejected. He was, he wrote, 'both a burden and a terror to myself, nor did I ever so know, as now, what it was to be weary of my life, and yet afraid to die'.

'I have loved you with an everlasting love.'

In his spiritual agony, Bunyan would receive some help from a Scripture verse but it lasted only a few days, or sometimes only a few hours, until another verse would condemn him. As he explained it, sometimes a verse from the Bible 'came into my heart, such a great word, it seemed to be writ in great letters', but then verses of judgment would come again. 'How many Scriptures are there against me!' Bunyan cried, and asked, 'Which of them would get the better of me?' For a long time this battle of the texts continued, until his soul was like a 'broken vessel, driven as with the winds'.

Bunyan's fears worsened when he read the life of Francis Spira, a sixteenth-century Italian who recanted his Protestantism under pressure from the Inquisition. Spira died in despair, saying that he had denied Christ, lost all faith, and was possessed by 'legions of demons'.[11] In his depression Bunyan found that this book was like rubbing salt into a wound. He was sorry that God had made him a man. I 'counted the estate of everything that God had made far better than this dreadful state of mine,' Bunyan wrote. 'Yea, gladly would I have been in the condition of dog or horse.'

Bunyan believed that his sin 'was bigger than the sins of a country, of a kingdom, or of the whole world'. With great bitterness of soul he said to himself, 'How can God comfort such a wretch as I?' Yet 'I had no sooner said it,' Bunyan wrote, 'but this returned upon me, as an echo answers a voice, "This sin is not unto death."' With these words, Bunyan felt that he had been 'raised out of a grave'. A little later, another verse—'I have loved you with an everlasting love'—brought even more relief and hope. It was as if God was saying to him, 'I loved you while you were committing this sin, I loved you before, I love you still, and I will love you forever.'

'My grace is sufficient for you.'

Bunyan 'was constantly seeking and was ready to grasp any vestige of hope. But even in his most miserable moments he wanted truth rather than comfort.'[12] He repeated the words 'My grace is sufficient for you', but felt that this verse was 'not large enough' for him. He was not sure that the words 'for you' really included him. 'But one day as I was in a meeting of God's people, full of sadness and terror,' he wrote, 'these words did, with great power, suddenly break in upon me, "My grace is sufficient for you, my grace is sufficient for you, my grace is sufficient for you", three times together; and, oh! I thought that every word was a mighty word to me. It broke my heart and filled me full of joy.' He was now convinced that the verse 'had arms of grace so wide that it could not only enclose me, but many more besides'.

At last the miserable words and his fear about Esau's selling his birthright began to weaken, and Scripture verses declaring 'the sufficiency of grace prevailed with peace and joy'. Still his mental and spiritual struggles were not over. He envied the trust of the people of the Bedford church. 'Ah, how safely did I see them walk, whom God had hedged in! They were within his care. Now did those blessed places that spoke of God's keeping his people shine like the sun before me, though not to comfort me.' Bunyan was tormented by thoughts of Peter's failure and, even worse, the betrayal of Judas. He wrote, 'My peace would be in and out sometimes twenty times a day: comfort now, and trouble presently; peace now, and before I could go a furlong, as full of fear and guilt as ever heart could hold.'

'Your righteousness is in heaven.'

Henri Talon writes that Bunyan 'still went through hours of torment ... But joy beat within the sadness, and the union of these two gave his soul its characteristic note.'[13] He remembered each verse of Scripture and each thought as he made his way from fear and doubt to assurance of salvation. The words of Hebrews 13:5—'I will never leave you nor forsake you'—gave him hope. 'O Lord,' Bunyan said, 'but I have left you. Then it answered again, "But I will not leave you."'

Fresh and saving insights came more and more to Bunyan, as he searched the Bible, enlightened by the Spirit. He was enabled to look away from his spiritual accomplishments, or lack of them, to his heavenly treasure. One day these words came to him with great power: 'Your righteousness is in heaven.' Bunyan wrote, 'Now I could look from myself to him, and should reckon that all those graces of God that now were green in me, were yet but like those cracked groats and fourpence—halfpennies that rich men carry in their purses, when their gold is in their trunks at home! Oh, I saw my gold was in my trunk at home! In Christ, my Lord and Saviour!'

Still he could not escape fully those 'terrible scriptures' that condemned him. Then he remembered the words in James 2:13, 'Mercy rejoices against judgment.' This was a 'wonderment' to him, as he came to realize that 'the word of the law and wrath must give place to the word of life and grace'. He was learning to take individual Bible verses in their context, and to understand the whole message of the Bible. He rejoiced to find that 'the Scriptures could agree in the salvation of his soul'. He understood that 'the word of the law and wrath must give place to the word of life and grace; because though the word of condemnation be glorious, yet the word of life and salvation far exceeds in glory'. He now saw the purpose in the condemning verses because they led him away from his own work to the 'heights and depths in grace, and love, and mercy'. 'Great sins do draw out great grace,' he wrote, 'and where guilt is most terrible and fierce, there the mercy of God in Christ appears most high and mighty.' In *Come and Welcome to Jesus Christ*, Bunyan stated that conversion comes primarily not from 'the overheavy load of sin, but the discovery of mercy; not the roaring of the devil, but the drawing of the Father, that makes a man come to Jesus Christ'.

'O now I know, I know!'

One day, sitting by the fire, Bunyan 'suddenly felt' this desire sound in his heart, 'I must go to Jesus.' 'At this my former darkness and atheism fled away, and the blessed things of heaven were set within my view,' he wrote. With great joy he told his wife, 'O now I know, I know!' He would spend the rest of his life teaching and preaching and living the good news of God's grace in Christ that he had heard and finally believed.

With *'great fear and trembling', I began to preach 'the blessed gospel'.*

For some time now Bunyan had worshipped with 'the poor people in Bedford'. He had listened as John Gifford taught the Bible and conferred with the people 'about the dealings of God with the soul'. In 1655 Bunyan joined Gifford's church; his name stands nineteenth on its roll of members. He was baptized—even though he had been baptized as an infant a few days old in the Church of England at Elstow— in the waters of the River Great Ouse, which flows through Bedford.

Five or six years after Bunyan was 'awakened', the leaders of the Bedford church, seeing that God had enabled him to 'see both the want and worth of Jesus Christ our Lord', asked him to speak 'a word of exhortation unto them'. 'They were both affected and comforted,' Bunyan wrote, 'and gave thanks to the Father of mercies for the grace bestowed on me.' Like both Calvin and Knox, Bunyan was at first reluctant to 'make use of his gifts in an open way'. But, with 'great fear and trembling' and knowledge of his 'own weakness', he began to preach 'that blessed gospel' that God had shown him 'in the holy word of truth'.

John Bunyan not only preached to the people in the Bedford church, he became an evangelist and a missionary. He wrote that he preached to both 'them that believed, but also to those who had not yet received the faith'. His ministry, he said, was 'to get into the darkest places in the country because I found my spirit leaned most after awakening and converting work'. Hundreds came to hear the tinker who had become a preacher, and many responded to his message. He wrote: 'I had not preached long before some began to be touched by the word and to be greatly afflicted in their minds at the apprehension of the greatness of their sin and of their need of Jesus Christ.'

For some time, however, Bunyan was plagued with feelings of guilt and terror that accompanied him to the very door of the pulpit. At times when he prepared to preach upon 'some smart and scorching portion of the word', Satan suggested, 'What, will you preach this? This condemns yourself.' Sometimes he was 'violently assaulted with thoughts of blasphemy and strongly tempted to speak the words before the congregation'. Bunyan pictured his own experience in *Pilgrim's Progress*. Christian's greatest trial comes when one of the wicked ones from the burning pit creeps up behind him and whispers 'many grievous blasphemies to him, which he thought had proceeded from his own mind'. Like Christian, Bunyan at first 'had not the discretion either to stop his ears or to know from where these blasphemies came'.

'The persecution that always attends the word fell upon the church.'

Oliver Cromwell died in 1658, and on May 8, 1660, Parliament proclaimed Charles II as king. The new monarch led England into a riot of spending, splendour, pleasure, gaiety, and lasciviousness. During the Commonwealth there had been a measure of religious freedom, when most of the godly had lived side by side 'in argumentative peace'.[14] This liberty ended, as king and Parliament now sought to re-establish a single state church controlled from above, and preaching tinkers with undesirable views were silenced. 'The persecution that always attends the word fell upon the church,' Bunyan wrote.

'I must do it, I must do it.'

On November 12, 1660, Bunyan planned to preach to a group of people in Lower Samsell, Bedfordshire. A friend told him that a warrant had been issued for his arrest, charging that he had 'devilishly and perniciously abstained from coming to the parish church to hear divine service, and was a common upholder of several unlawful meetings and conventicles, to the great disturbance and distraction of the good subjects of this kingdom'. Bunyan knew that he could be arrested for preaching, but he also knew that he had to preach. He believed that if he did not preach he would cause his 'weak and newly converted brethren' to be discouraged. When his friends warned him of the danger and urged him to desist, he said, 'No, by no means. Come, be of good cheer, let us not be daunted; our cause is good, we need not be ashamed.' He opened the meeting with prayer. As he began to preach, the constable arrived and arrested him for calling together the people and 'holding unlawful meetings and conventicles'.

The local magistrate offered Bunyan a way out: if he would go home and not preach anymore, he would not be prosecuted. This Bunyan would not promise, so he was hauled away and locked up in the Bedford jail. Bunyan felt that he 'was as a man who was pulling down his house upon the head of his wife and children', yet, he said, 'I must do it, I must do it.' He was sentenced to three months in prison, after which he would have to cease preaching and attend services in the Church of England or else be banished from the realm. He was warned that should he return without the monarch's permission after being exiled, he would be hanged. Bunyan refused to be intimidated. He told the authorities, 'If I was out of prison today I would preach the gospel again tomorrow, by the help of God.'

For most of the next twelve years Bunyan remained in the Bedford jail, in filthy, overcrowded conditions, sadly separated from his wife and children, for no other crime than that of preaching. He slept on straw in a cold cell with no fireplace. In one of his books, a book on prayer, he wrote: 'When I have been in my fits of agonies of spirit, I have been strongly persuaded to leave off, and to seek the Lord no longer; but being made to understand what great sinners the Lord has had mercy upon, and how large his promises were still to sinners; and that it was not the whole, but the sick, not the righteous, but the sinner, not the full, but the empty, that he extended his grace and mercy unto—this made me, through the assistance of his Holy Spirit, to cleave to him, to hang upon him, and yet to cry, though for the present he made no answer.'

'Yet by the faith of Christ I can mount higher than the stars.'

In prison Bunyan's faith and courage grew. He wrote: 'When God makes the bed he must be easy who is cast thereon; a blessed pillow has that man for his head, though to all beholders it is hard as a stone. He can make a jail more beautiful than a palace, restraint more sweet by far than liberty, and the reproach of Christ greater riches than the treasures of Egypt.'

In *Prison Meditations* Bunyan wrote:

For though men keep my outward man
    within their locks and bars,
yet by the faith of Christ I can
    mount higher than the stars.

For, as the devil sets before
    me heaviness and grief,
so God sets Christ and grace much more,
    Whereby I take relief.

God sometimes visits prisons more
    than lordly palaces.
He often knocketh at our door,
    when he their houses miss.

'He dares not leave preaching.'

Bunyan protested against his imprisonment, but he
would not promise to conform to the Church of England
and give up preaching. He maintained that the powers
that be are ordained by God and must be obeyed, but that
neither obedience nor authority should be absolute. He
was firm but respectful in his dealings with the authorities.
He closed the account of his defence before a 'Clerk of the
Peace': "'Sir, the law has provided two ways of obeying. The
one to do that which I, in my conscience, do believe that I
am bound to do, actively, and where I cannot obey actively,
there I am willing to lie down, and to suffer what they shall
do to me." At this he sat still, and said no more. I did thank

him for his civil and meek discoursing with me, and so we parted. O that we might meet in heaven!'

Elizabeth, Bunyan's second wife, travelled to London with a petition seeking her husband's release. She was articulate, resourceful, and courageous, and she possessed a working knowledge of the law. When it was obvious that she was not going to succeed in gaining a judicial review, she went to the Swan Chamber, where two judges sat with justices and people of the gentry. Elizabeth told the judges (in what Christopher Hill calls a 'final magnificent explosion') that because her husband was 'a tinker, and a poor man, therefore he was despised, and could not have justice'.[15] When one of the judges asked Elizabeth, 'Will your husband leave preaching?' she answered, 'He dares not leave preaching.' John Brown comments, 'Elizabeth Bunyan was simply an English peasant woman: could she have spoken with more dignity had she been a crowned queen?'[16]

'To live upon God who is invisible.'

Two great concerns troubled Bunyan as he faced a long time in prison. The first was 'How to be able to endure'. But he learned to pray to be 'strengthened with all might, according to God's glorious power, unto all patience and longsuffering with joyfulness'. The second was 'How to be able to encounter death', should that be his 'portion'. Second Corinthians 1:9 made him understand that, like Paul, he should not trust in himself but 'in God which raises the dead'. And

2 Corinthians 4:18 taught him, as Bunyan put it, 'to live upon God who is invisible'.[17] Whatever happened, Bunyan determined to commit everything, life and death, to God: 'Wherefore, thought I, the point being thus, I am for going on, and venturing my eternal state with Christ, whether I have comfort here or no; if God does not come in, thought I, I will leap off the ladder even blindfold into eternity, sink or swim, come heaven, come hell; Lord Jesus, if you will catch me, do; if not, I will venture for your name.'

Bunyan hoped that if he should be put to death, he would be allowed to speak some words to people who would come to see him die. If God would convert but one soul through his last message, he wrote, he would 'not count his life thrown away, nor lost'.

'Many hardships, miseries and wants.'

In jail Bunyan suffered deeply the separation from his wife and children. Parting from them, he wrote, 'has oft been to me in this place as the pulling the flesh from my bones'. He thought of 'the many hardships, miseries and wants' that his poor family would face, especially his beloved blind daughter, now ten years old. Bunyan wrote: 'Poor child, thought I, what sorrow are you like to have for your portion in this world? You must be beaten, must beg, suffer hunger, cold, nakedness, and a thousand calamities, though I cannot now endure the wind should blow upon you; but yet, thought I, I must venture you all with God.'

When his daughter Mary died in 1663, Bunyan began a book called *The Resurrection of the Dead*, taking comfort in the hope of the resurrection, as Luther did when his daughter Magdalena died. Bunyan completed the book in 1665 while the plague raged in England. He wrote that 'this doctrine of the resurrection of the dead has that power, both to bear up and to awe; both to encourage and to keep within compass, the spirit and body of the people of God'. He explained: 'Though God's saints have felt the power of much of his grace, and have had many a sweet word fulfilled on them; yet one word will be unfulfilled so long as the grave can shut her mouth upon them: but, as I said before, when the gates of death do open before them, and the bars of the grave do fall asunder; then shall be brought to pass that saying that is written, "Death is swallowed up of victory"; and then will they hear that most pleasant voice, "Awake and sing, you that dwell in dust: for your dew is as the dew of herbs, and the earth shall cast out the dead."'

Elizabeth Bunyan, who lost her first child after premature labour brought on by her husband's arrest, was left with the care of his four children 'with nothing to live on but the charity of good people', as she told one of her husband's judges. To help support his family Bunyan worked in prison by making 'many hundred gross of long tagg'd laces'. Bunyan found comfort in the words of Jeremiah 49:11, 'Leave your fatherless children, I will preserve them alive, and let your widows trust in me.' Bunyan dearly loved his first and second wives and his six children. He wrote: 'I love to play the child with little children, and I learned something by so doing.' He wrote *A Book for Boys and Girls*, which was a series of little pictures familiar to children, to which he added Christian application. For example:

> The water is the fish's element;
> leave her but there, and she is well content.
> So's he, who in the path of life doth plod,
> take all, says he, let me but have my God.
>
> This pretty bird, O! how she flies and sings,
> but could she do so if she had not wings?
> Her wings bespeak my faith, her songs my peace;
> when I believe and sing my doubtings cease.
>
> Poor silly mole, that thou should'st love to be
> where thou nor sun, nor moon, nor stars can see.
> But O! how silly's he who doth not care
> so he gets earth, to have of heaven a share!

A Book for Boys and Girls shows Bunyan 'at his best and most adventurous as a poet, and expresses more completely the many sides of his personality', such as his love for children, his gentleness, his country ways, and keen observation of animals and plants. Richard Greaves comments, 'Given the fact that it includes poetic versions of the Ten Commandments, the Lord's Prayer, and the [Apostles'] Creed, as well as poems on the sacraments, Christ's love, the spouse of Christ, and human nature, *A Book for Boys and Girls* served almost as a catechism in verse.'[18]

'I never had in all my life so great an inlet into the word of God as now.'

As Bunyan began his time in prison, his church entered a season of trouble. Expelled in September 1660 from the parish church building, where it had occupied a central place in the town's religious life, the church now met in members' houses. Seventeenth-century English jails were often casually run, and Bunyan was given occasional liberty. He used these opportunities to visit his family and to preach in Bedford and the surrounding area—even as far afield as London. 'An awakening word' was what he hoped to bring to people. He 'was not altogether without hopes' that his imprisonment might be 'an awakening to the saints in the country'.

Bunyan spent much of his time in prison studying and writing. His Bible was his treasure, and almost his only book. His trouble took him deeper into the meaning of Scripture. He wrote: 'I have received, among many things, much conviction, instruction, and understanding. I never had in all my life so great an inlet into the word of God as now. Scriptures that I saw nothing in before are made in this place and state to shine upon me; Jesus Christ also was never more real and apparent than now.'

'I dreamed a dream.'

As the months passed, Bunyan's spirits sank. There were many weeks in which he was 'in a very sad and low condition'. 'Depression can recur,' writes Richard Greaves, 'and it is likely that he once again battled the illness in late 1663 and 1664 as the bleak years in prison took their toll.'[19] One day, when it was Bunyan's turn to preach to his friends in their prison chamber, he found himself 'so empty, spiritless, and barren' that he thought he would not be able to speak so much as five words of truth 'with life and evidence'. Then his eye fell on the description of the New Jerusalem in Revelation 21:11, and he preached with power. 'While distributing the truth, it did so increase in his hand' that, 'of the fragments, he gathered up a basketful', which he later expanded into a book called *The Holy City*.

As time went on, Bunyan's situation began to look more hopeful. He was released from prison for a brief time during 1666, possibly owing to the threat of plague. Late in 1667 he began expanding a sermon into a book entitled *The Heavenly Foot-Man: or, a Description of the Man That Gets to Heaven*. While he was working on this book, he fell 'suddenly into an allegory', as he put it, and was moved to write a quite different kind of book. He explained:

> Thus I set pen to paper with delight,
> and quickly had my thoughts on black and white.
> For having now my method by the end,
> still as I pull'd, it came.[20]

When Bunyan sought advice from friends concerning publishing a book of this kind, 'some said, "John, print it"; others said, "Not so." Some said, "It might do good", others said, "No."' Fortunately, Bunyan decided to print it, with sage advice to his critics that they wait and see if it proved useful. It did! Bunyan's deep experience of his own sinful heart and God's abounding grace, his thorough knowledge of Scripture, and his fertile imagination combined to produce one of the world's greatest books, *The Pilgrim's Progress*. It was Bunyan's own testimony once again. 'He had only to translate his spiritual odyssey into an allegory,' wrote Roger Sharrock.[21] John Bunyan ended his poetic 'Apology' with an engaging invitation to the reader:

> —O then come hither,
> and lay my book, your head, and heart together.

The opening sentences of *The Pilgrim's Progress* are among the most memorable in English literature: 'As I walked through the wilderness of this world, I lighted on a certain place, where was a den; and I laid me down in that place to sleep: And as I slept, I dreamed a dream.'

In its opening pages Bunyan wrote these words about himself:

> O world of wonders! (I can say no less)
> that I should be preserv'd in that distress
> that I have met with here! O blessed be
> that hand that from it hath delivered me.

Yes, snares, and pits, and traps, and nets did lie
my path about, that worthless silly I
might have been catch'd, intangled, and cast down:
but since I live, let Jesus wear the crown.

There are many places in *The Pilgrim's Progress* in which we find Bunyan's 'testimony'. One such is the exchange between Hopeful and Christian. Christian asks Hopeful how he first came to seek the good of his soul. Hopeful describes how he was taken up with the treasures and riches of the world until he heard the truth from 'beloved Faithful' and Christian at Vanity Fair. For some time he struggled under conviction of sin before he decided to mend his life by forsaking sin and his sinful friends and give himself to good works. But he came to realize that all his good works were 'as filthy rags'. He did not know what to do until he spoke to Faithful, who told him that unless he could 'obtain the righteousness of a man that never had sinned', neither his own righteousness nor 'all the righteousness of the world' could save him. Faithful taught him a prayer that Hopeful prayed again and again until the Father showed him his Son. Hopeful further explained:

'I did not see him with my bodily eyes, but with the eyes of my understanding, and thus it was: One day I was very sad, I think sadder than any one time in my life, and this sadness was through a fresh sight of the greatness and vileness of my sins. And as I was then looking for nothing but hell, and the everlasting damnation of my soul, suddenly, as I thought, I saw the Lord Jesus look down from heaven upon me, and saying, "Believe on the Lord Jesus Christ, and you shall be saved."

'But, I replied, "Lord, I am a great, a very great sinner." And he answered, "My grace is sufficient for you." Then I said, "But, Lord, what is believing?" And then I saw from that saying "He that comes to me shall never hunger, and he that believes on me shall never thirst", that believing and coming were all one; and that he that came, that is, ran out in his heart and affections after salvation by Christ, he indeed believed in Christ.'

Christian and Hopeful leave their rough and hard road for an easier way in nearby By-path Meadow. They soon realize their mistake and attempt to go back but fall into an exhausted sleep, and Giant Despair discovers them and hauls them away to Doubting Castle, where he locks them in a dungeon. 'In composing these terrible pages, Bunyan writes straight and bold out of his own heart and conscience,' commented Alexander Whyte. 'Last week,' he continued, 'I went over *Grace Abounding* again and marked the passages in which its author describes his own experiences of doubt, diffidence, and despair, till I gave over counting the passages, they are so many.'[22]

'I tell you, I would be, and hope I am, a Christian.'

After 1668 Bunyan's imprisonment seems to have become more and more nominal. He was able to take on an increasing load of church work, culminating in his election as pastor of the Bedford congregation on December 21, 1671. In 1672 King Charles II issued a Declaration of Indulgence for both Protestant Dissenters and Roman Catholics, and in March Bunyan was released from prison. Among the few possessions he carried home was probably an incomplete manuscript of *The Pilgrim's Progress*.

As pastor of the Bedford church Bunyan sought to be faithful to the Bible and to the essentials of the gospel, but, as he said, he never cared 'to meddle with things that were controverted, and in dispute among the saints, especially things of the lowest nature'. His views on church government reflected both Congregational and Baptist convictions. When Baptists pressed Bunyan to declare to which group he belonged, he replied, 'Since you would know by what name I would be distinguished from others; I tell you, I would be, and hope I am, a Christian.' Bunyan defended 'the godly in the land that are not of our persuasion'. He wrote that 'thousands of thousands' who did not hold the views of the Baptists 'acquitted themselves and their Christianity before men and are now with the innumerable company of angels and the spirits of men made perfect'. To his Baptist critics Bunyan replied 'that the church of Christ has not warrant to keep out of their communion the Christian that is discovered to be a visible saint by the word, the Christian that walks according to his light with God'. In his *All Loves Excelling: The Saints' Knowledge of Christ's*

Love, Bunyan wrote that those who know the love of Christ which passes knowledge are those 'that *sweeten* churches, and that bring glory to God and to religion'. He added that such people 'are, at this day, wanting in the churches'.

'Home to prison again.'

Uncertainties in government policy led to inconsistency in the execution of the laws against Dissenters. The bishops advised the king to suppress the conventicles (the religious meetings of Dissenters), and all licences issued under the declaration were recalled. Because Bunyan had not taken communion at the parish church as required by law, he had to go 'home to prison again'. Bunyan spent six more months in jail before being released again in June 1677. It was during his second imprisonment that he revised *Grace Abounding* for its fourth edition and completed *The Pilgrim's Progress*, which was published in 1678. Part Two of *The Pilgrim's Progress* was not published until 1684.

'I would willingly exchange my learning for the tinker's power of touching men's hearts.'

After his brief second imprisonment in 1677, Bunyan lived another decade. He did not add further to *Grace Abounding*; however he did set forth his testimony in his sermons. Only occasionally, however, did he refer directly to himself. As a Puritan preacher he was devoted above all to the explanation and application of the Scriptures. But in doing that, Bunyan tirelessly expounded the truths that had captured his heart and changed his life.

Bunyan became a recognized leader among the dissenting churches in his part of England. Because of his influence and popularity, some, though often in a jeering way, referred to him as 'Bishop Bunyan'. When a Cambridge professor challenged the right of a tinker to preach, a Baptist friend defended Bunyan, pointing out his ability 'to mend souls as well as pots and pans'.[23] It is recorded that King Charles II asked John Owen, the distinguished Puritan theologian and Oxford scholar, how such an educated man as he could sit and listen to a tinker. Owen replied, 'I would willingly exchange my learning for the tinker's power of touching men's hearts.'[24]

Bunyan's 'simple themes, homely anecdotes, colloquial language, and abundant repetition', as well as illustrations drawn from his own life, enabled him to hold congregations 'nearly spellbound'.[25]

At first, according to Bunyan's own testimony, he cried out 'against men's sins, and their fearful state because of them'. 'The terrors of the law, and guilt for my transgressions, lay heavy on my conscience.' But God gave him 'many sweet discoveries of his blessed grace', and Bunyan changed his way of preaching. He now preached 'Jesus Christ in all his offices, relations, and benefits unto the world'. Next, Bunyan recorded, 'God led me into something of the mystery of union with Christ.' All his sermons, said Bunyan, contained 'these three chief points of the word of God'—our sin and guilt, salvation through Jesus, and union with Christ.

'God has been merciful to me and has kept me.'

Bunyan resisted temptations toward 'pride and liftings up of heart'. He believed that he had gifts for ministry, but he knew that he also 'had cause to walk humbly with God, and be little in his own eyes, and to remember that his gifts were not his own, but the church's'. He wrote, 'Gifts indeed are desirable, but yet great grace and small gifts are better than great gifts and no grace.' The power and blessing in his preaching came from God. He wrote: 'Sometimes when I have thought I did no good, then I did the most of all; and at other times when I thought I should catch them I have fished for nothing.'

Satan tried, Bunyan wrote, to overthrow his ministry, not only by tempting him to pride, but also by 'slanders and reproaches'. He was greatly hurt when he was unjustly accused of sexual immorality. He answered these charges in a later edition of *Grace Abounding*. He refused to take credit for a life that had been blameless in this respect, and ended his refutation of the charges against him with 'an ascription of praise to God'. 'Not that I have been thus kept because of any goodness in me more than any other, but to whom I pray that he will keep me still, not only from this, but from every evil way and work, and preserve me to his heavenly kingdom.'

Saved by Grace

A brief sampling of John Bunyan's sermons and other writings presents the Bible's gracious message to sinners and illustrates his own testimony. His sermons and books are a transcript of Bunyan's own heart; for God was still blessing him by grace and shaping him by his word. He continued to preach what he 'smartingly did feel'.

In the books he wrote, almost all of which were developed from his sermons, Bunyan repeated, emphasized, and celebrated God's grace.

In *The Law and Grace Unfolded*, he exclaims: 'O, when a God of grace is upon a throne of grace, and a poor sinner stands by and begs for grace, and that in the name of a gracious Christ, in and by the help of the Spirit of grace, can it be otherwise but that such a sinner must obtain mercy and grace to help in time of need? O, then, come boldly.'

In *Saved by Grace* Bunyan sets forth both the Reformed doctrine of predestination (the teaching that God chooses some for salvation or, as Bunyan put it, the fact that God 'appointed them their portion and measure of grace, and that before the world began') and God's urgent calling upon sinners to believe and repent. What holds these two apparently contradictory tenets together for Bunyan is God's grace—God's grace in choosing and God's grace in inviting the lost to come, grace that dazzles the angels and astonishes devils. 'O sinner, will you not open? Behold, God the Father and his Son, Jesus Christ, stand both at the door of your heart, beseeching there for favour from you, that you will be reconciled to them, with promise, if you will comply, to forgive you all your sins. O grace! O amazing grace! To see a prince entreat a beggar to receive an alms would be a strange sight; to see a king entreat the traitor to accept of mercy would be a stranger sight than that; but to see God entreat a sinner, to hear Christ say, "I stand at the door and knock", with a heart full and a heaven full of grace to bestow upon him that opens, this is such a sight as dazzles the eyes of angels.'

The grace of God that saves the elect and invites the sinner is the grace of the Holy Trinity—the Father, the Son, and the Holy Spirit. Bunyan described the grace of God the Son in the following eloquent passage: 'Son of the Blessed, what grace was manifest in your condescension! Grace brought you down from heaven, grace stripped you of your glory, grace made you poor and despicable, grace made you bear such burdens of sin, such burdens of sorrow, such burdens of God's curse as are unspeakable. O Son of God! Grace was in all your tears, grace came bubbling out of your side with your blood, grace came forth with every word of your sweet mouth. Grace came out where the whip smote you, where the thorns pricked you, where the nails and spear pierced you. O blessed Son of God! Here is grace indeed! Unsearchable riches of grace! Unthought-of riches of grace! Grace to make angels wonder, grace to make sinners happy, grace to astonish devils.'

Come, and Welcome to Jesus Christ

Come, and Welcome to Jesus Christ, a beautiful book with music in its title, grew from a sermon on words that had helped to heal Bunyan's own spiritual wounds: 'All that the Father gives me shall come to me; and him that comes to me I will in no wise cast out' (John 6:37). Bunyan wrote: 'They that are coming to Jesus Christ are often heartily afraid that Jesus Christ will not receive them. But this word "in no wise" cuts the throat of all objections; and it was dropped by the Lord Jesus for that very end; and to help the faith that is mixed with unbelief. And it is, as it were, the sum of all promises; neither can any objection be made upon the unworthiness that you find in you, that this promise will not assuage.

'But I am a great sinner, say you.

'"I will in no wise cast out," says Christ.

'But I am an old sinner, say you.

'"I will in no wise cast out," says Christ.

'But I am a hard-hearted sinner, say you.

'"I will in no wise cast out," says Christ.

'But I am a backsliding sinner, say you.

'"I will in no wise cast out," says Christ.

'But I have served Satan all my days, say you.

'"I will in no wise cast out," says Christ.

'But I have sinned against light, say you.

'"I will in no wise cast out," says Christ.

'But I have sinned against mercy, say you.

'"I will in no wise cast out," says Christ.

'But I have no good thing to bring with me, say you.

'"I will in no wise cast out," says Christ.'

The Jerusalem Sinner Saved

In one of his last writings, *The Jerusalem Sinner Saved, or Good News for the Vilest of Men*, Bunyan expounded Luke 24:47, where Christ commands his disciples to preach repentance and forgiveness of sins to all nations beginning in Jerusalem. Stressing that the offer of mercy was extended first to the greatest sinners—'Jerusalem sinners', he called them—he put himself among them: 'I would say to my soul, "O my soul! this is not the place of despair; this is not the time to despair in; as long as mine eyes can find a promise in the Bible, as long as there is the least mention of grace, as long as there is a moment left me of breath or life in this world, so long will I wait or look for mercy, so long will I fight against unbelief and despair."'

'Hold fast till I come.'

Again Bunyan told his story—the story of God's grace—in another allegory, *The Holy War*, published in 1682. In the words of Marcus Loane, Bunyan's 'own experience had made him a master of the human heart and all its feelings. The City of Mansoul had no nook or lane to which he was a stranger, and well he knew the sound of the Enemy's Drum.'[26]

Bunyan again supplies words of personal testimony:

> For my part, I myself was in the town,
> both when 'twas set up, and when pulling down;
> I saw Diabolus in his possession,
> and Mansoul under his oppression.
> Yea, I was there when she own'd him for lord
> and to him did submit with one accord.

About Emmanuel's recovery of Mansoul, Bunyan wrote:

> What is here in view
> of mine own knowledge I dare say is true.
> I saw the Prince's armed men come down,
> by troops, by thousands, to besiege the town.
> I saw the captains, heard the trumpets sound,
> and how his forces covered all the ground.
> Yea, how they set themselves in battle-ray,
> I shall remember to my dying day.

Emmanuel's words end the book and contain Bunyan's own testimony: 'Remember O my Mansoul that you are beloved of me; as I have therefore taught you to watch, to fight, to pray, and to make war against my foes, so now I command you to believe that my love is constant to you. O my Mansoul, how I have set my heart, my love, upon you; watch. Behold, I lay none other burden upon you than what you have already. Hold fast till I come.'

Paul's Departure and Crown

In *Paul's Departure and Crown*, Bunyan exhorted the godly to stand firm in the gospel. 'The great and chief design of God in sending us into the world, especially in converting us and possessing our souls with gifts and graces,' Bunyan wrote, is 'that we might be to the glory of his grace.' No work of Bunyan is more directed to his fellow ministers than this one. He exhorts them to 'a diligent watchfulness' and 'a diligent preaching of the word of the Lord'.

'I see myself now at the end of my journey.'

In 1684 Bunyan published Part Two of *The Pilgrim's Progress*, just a few years before his death in 1688. The book ends with the words of Mr Stand-fast as he crossed the river and entered the Celestial City, words that beautifully present Bunyan's own sure hope of heaven: 'I see myself now at the end of my journey, my toilsome days are ended. I am going now to see that head that was crowned with thorns, and that face that was spit upon for me. I have formerly lived by hearsay and faith; but now I go where I shall live by sight, and shall be with him in whose company I delight myself. I have loved to hear my Lord spoken of; and wherever I have seen the print of his shoe in the earth, there I have coveted to set my foot too. His name has been to me as a civet-box;[27] yea, sweeter than all perfumes. His voice too has been most sweet; and his countenance I have more desired than they that have most desired the light of the sun.'

'Do good for one another.'

In *The Saints' Privilege and Profit* Bunyan wrote, 'As there is mercy to be obtained by us at the throne of grace, for the pardon of all our sins, so there is also grace to be found that strengthens us more, to all good walking and living before him.' Bunyan not only preached grace, he practised it in 'good walking and living' before God.

In August 1688 Bunyan rode on horseback from Bedford to Reading to visit and seek to reconcile a father and son who had quarrelled. Travelling on to London in heavy rain, he was drenched and fell sick with a violent fever. One of Bunyan's biographers aptly stated: 'Thus one last act of love and charity put an end to a life almost entirely devoted to the good of others.'[28]

Toward the end of what was to be his last sermon, John Bunyan preached: 'If you are the children of God, live together lovingly; if the world quarrel with you, it is no matter; but it is sad if you quarrel together; if this be amongst you, it is a sign of ill-breeding; it is not according to the rules you have in the word of God. Do you see a soul that has the image of God in him? Love him, love him; say, This man and I must go to heaven one day; serve one another, do good for one another; and if any wrong you, pray to God to right you, and love the brotherhood. Consider that the holy God is your Father, and let this oblige you to live like the children of God, that you may look your Father in the face, with comfort, another day.'

'*I go to the Father of our Lord Jesus Christ.*'

That day was not far off for John Bunyan. His last words were 'all brief and succinct and full of the spiritual wisdom for which he was famous', writes Marcus Loane.[29] Many of these were recorded and appear in *The Works of John Bunyan*, including this one: 'Weep not for me, but for yourselves. I go to the Father of our Lord Jesus Christ, who will, no doubt, through the mediation of his blessed Son, receive me, though a sinner; where I hope we before long shall meet, to sing a new song, and remain everlastingly happy, world without end. Amen.'

John Bunyan died on August 31, 1688. He was not quite sixty years old, the author, it was said, of sixty books. He was buried in Bunhill Fields, London, the Dissenters' graveyard. The Bedford church-book records the stunned reaction of his congregation: 'Wednesday the 4th of September was kept in prayer and humiliation for this heavy stroke upon us, the death of dear brother Bunyan.'

Elizabeth survived her husband by only a few years. She died in 1691, 'to follow her faithful pilgrim from this world to the other, whither he was gone before her'.[30]

'The Song of a Pilgrim.'

In Part Two of *The Pilgrim's Progress*, Mr Valiant-for-truth and Mr Great-Heart join the other pilgrims in the final stages of their journey from the City of Destruction to the Celestial City. Great-Heart thrilled the company when he sang 'The Song of a Pilgrim'. In it Bunyan sings his own testimony:

> He who would valiant be
>   'gainst all disaster,
> let him in constancy
>   follow the Master.
> There's no discouragement
>   shall make him once relent
> his first avowed intent
>   to be a pilgrim.
>
> Who so beset him round
>   with dismal stories,
> do but themselves confound,
>   his strength the more is.
> No foes shall stay his might,
>   though he with giants fight;
> he will make good his right
>   to be a pilgrim.
>
> Since, Lord, thou dost defend
>   us with thy Spirit,
> We know we at the end
>   shall life inherit.

Then fancies flee away!
I'll fear not what men say,
I'll labour night and day
to be a pilgrim.

Endnotes

[1] Christopher Hill, *A Tinker and a Poor Man: John Bunyan and His Church, 1628-1688* (New York: W. W. Norton & Co., 1988), 4.

[2] Marcus L. Loane, *Makers of Puritan History* (1960; repr. Edinburgh: Banner of Truth Trust, 2009), 126.

[3] Rebecca S. Beal, '*Grace Abounding to the Chief of Sinners*: John Bunyan's Pauline Epistle', in *Studies in English Literature, 1500-1900* (Baltimore: Johns Hopkins University Press, 1981), 148.

[4] Alexander Whyte, *Bunyan Characters: Bunyan Himself as Seen in His Grace Abounding* (Edinburgh: Oliphant, Anderson & Ferrier, n.d.), 245.

[5] Henri Talon, *John Bunyan: The Man and His Works* (Cambridge, MA: Harvard University Press, 1951), 45.

[6] In this game a player hits a piece of wood with a stick, making it fly into the air, where he strikes it again, driving it as far as he can.

[7] Talon, *John Bunyan*, 53.

[8] Michael A. Mullett, *John Bunyan in Context* (Keele, Staffordshire: Keele University Press, 1966), 30.

[9] Talon, *John Bunyan*, 63.

[10] Loane, *Makers of Puritan History*, 114. There is in Bedford a ten-foot bronze statue of John Bunyan. He holds in his hands an open Bible. A broken chain lies at his feet, symbolizing his long struggle to preach the gospel. On the pedestal are inscribed these words

from his most famous book: 'He had eyes uplifted to heaven; The best of books in his hand; The law of truth was written upon his lips; He stood as if he pleaded with men.'

11 The reading of *A Relation of the Fearful Estate of Francis Spira in the Year 1548* was almost a tradition in certain Puritan circles. Richard Baxter warned that reading this book caused or increased melancholy in many.

12 Owen C. Watkins, 'John Bunyan and His Experience', in *Puritan Papers: Volume One (1956–1959)*, ed. D. Martyn Lloyd-Jones (Phillipsburg, NJ: Presbyterian and Reformed Publishing Co.), 134.

13 Talon, *John Bunyan*, 72.

14 Hill, *John Bunyan*, 114.

15 Hill, *John Bunyan*, 107.

16 John Brown, *John Bunyan (1628–1688): His Life, Times, and Work* (London: Hulbert Publishing Co., 1928), 149-50.

17 John Piper wrote, 'I have not found any phrase in Bunyan's writings that captures better the key to his life than this one: "To live upon God that is invisible."' John Piper, *The Hidden Smile of God: The Fruit of Affliction in the Lives of John Bunyan, William Cowper, and David Brainerd* (Wheaton: Crossway Books, 2001), 43.

18 Richard L. Greaves, *Glimpses of Glory: John Bunyan and English Dissent* (Stanford, CA: Stanford University Press, 2002), 539, 542.

19 Greaves, *Glimpses of Glory*, 176.

20 C. S. Lewis wrote, 'I doubt if we shall ever know more of the process called "inspiration" than those two monosyllables ["It came"] tell us.' 'The Vision of John Bunyan', in *Selected Literary Essays*, edited by Walter Hooper (Cambridge: Cambridge University Press, 1960), 147.

21 Roger Sharrock, *John Bunyan* (London: Macmillan, 1968), 54.

22 Whyte, *Bunyan Characters*, 225.

[23] Richard L. Greaves, 'Introduction' to John Bunyan's *The Doctrine of the Law and Grace Unfolded* and *I Will Pray with the Spirit* (Oxford: Clarendon Press, 1976), xxxix.

[24] Brown, *John Bunyan*, 366.

[25] Greaves, *Glimpses of Glory*, 593, 595.

[26] Loane, *Makers of Puritan History*, 115.

[27] A perfume obtained from a civet-cat, a small animal of North Africa. The perfume was regarded as especially precious and is often referred to by Shakespeare.

[28] Talon, *John Bunyan*, 14.

[29] Loane, *Makers of Puritan History*, 153.

[30] Loane writes that in *Pilgrim's Progress* 'Christiana may reflect his second wife, Elizabeth, in her vigorous strength of character, while the gentle Mercy may be a heart reminiscence of the wife of his youth' (*Makers of Puritan History*, 140).